Dear Lord, They Want ME to Teach the LESSON!

Shane Groth & John D. Schroeder

ABINGDON PRESS
Nashville

DEAR LORD, THEY WANT ME TO TEACH THE LESSON!

Copyright © 1995 by Shane Groth & John D. Schroeder

All rights reserved.
No part of this work may be reproduced or transmitted in any form or by any means, electronic or mechanical, including photocopying and recording, or by any information storage or retrieval system, except as may be expressly permitted by the 1976 Copyright Act or in writing from the publisher. Requests for permission should be addressed in writing to Abingdon Press, 201 Eighth Avenue South, Nashville, TN 37203.

This book is printed on acid-free, recycled paper.

Library of Congress Cataloging-in-Publication Data

Groth, Shane M.
    Dear Lord, they want me to teach the lesson! / Shane Groth & John D. Schroeder.
    p. cm.
    ISBN 0-687-00255-9
    1. Christian education of adults.   2. Bible—Study and teaching.
I. Schroeder , John D.   II. Title.
BV1488.G75   1995
268'.434—dc20   94-41348
                                                                                                                                      CIP

Scripture quotations are taken from the HOLY BIBLE, NEW INTERNATIONAL VERSION®. Copyright © 1973, 1978, 1984 by International Bible Society. Used by permission of Zondervan Publishing House. All rights reserved.

To my brothers in Christ,
Bill and Paul Schroeder
—J. S.

To my old friend, Joel Frank,
For his kind heart and generous spirit
—S. G.

95 96 97 98 99 00 01 02 03 04—10 9 8 7 6 5 4 3 2 1

MANUFACTURED IN THE UNITED STATES OF AMERICA

CONTENTS

INTRODUCTION.............................. 5
  Checklists................................ 7

26 Thematic Bible Studies

1. A God Who Gets His Hands Dirty: *Psalm 23*....... 9
2. Finding Room for Jesus: *Luke 2:1-20* 11
3. One Way: *Ephesians 4:1-6*..................... 13
4. Tuning In to God: *1 Samuel 3:1-10* 15
5. No One Is an Island: *Romans 14:7-9*.............. 17
6. God Works with Whatever Is Available:
    1 Kings 17:7-16 19
7. Chaotic Calm: *Psalm 46* 21
8. What's Love Got to Do with It?: *1 Cor. 13:1-13* 23
9. Rich Toward God: *Luke 12:13-21* 25
10. Wanted: Dead and Alive: *Colossians 3:1-4* 27
11. Where's the Other Half? *Genesis 2:4-25*.......... 29
12. Yo-Yo Christians: *1 Kings 19:1-8*................ 31
13. Everything You Need to Know About Love:
    1 John 4:7-12 33
14. Conquerors or Conquistadors? *Romans 8:35-39*.... 35
15. Helping Hands: *Luke 7:11-17*................... 37
16. Living the Question: *Matthew 16:13-20* 39
17. Getting Honest with God: *Psalm 13*.............. 41
18. Subversive Joy: *Philippians 4:4-7*................ 43
19. Big Protection: *Psalm 91:1-4*................... 45
20. Where Does It Hurt? *Matthew 9:9-13*............. 47
21. Into the Darkness . . . : *Luke 22:39-62* 49
22. Risks and Rewards: *Matthew 20:17-28*........... 51
23. New Bones: *Ezekiel 37:1-14* 53

Contents

24. Sheep and Goats: *Matthew 25:31-46* 55
25. An Uncomfortable Faith: *Luke 4:14-28* 57
26. The Good in Good-bye: *John 14:1-12* 59

26 Bible Studies on Current Issues by Topic

27. Addiction: *Learning About Compulsive Behavior* 61
28. AIDS: *Jesus Shows Love to an Outcast* 63
29. Anger: *Consequences and Cures* 65
30. Courage: *Faith Turned into Action* 67
31. Crime: *The Good Samaritan* 69
32. Decisions: *Advice from the Expert* 71
33. Diversity: *Practicing Acceptance* 73
34. Ethics: *Matters of Trust and Truth* 75
35. Focus: *Looking to God* 77
36. Friendship: *Loyalty: Ruth and Naomi* 79
37. Healing: *In the Hands of God* 81
38. Persistence: *Requests to a Father* 83
39. Possessions: *Living in the Land of Plenty* 85
40. Power: *The Calming of the Storm* 87
41. Prayer: *God Listens to Us* 89
42. Pride: *The First Shall Be Last* 91
43. Priorities: *Eliminating Distractions* 93
44. Safety: *Peter's Angel* 95
45. Simplicity: *Less Is Often More* 97
46. Talent: *Blessed to Be a Blessing* 99
47. Temptation: *Matters of Choice* 101
48. Time: *Christian Time Management* 103
49. Tomorrow: *Looking Toward the Future* 105
50. Trouble: *Moving Our Mountains* 107
51. Unemployment: *Advice for Survival* 109
52. Worry: *Consider the Lilies* 111

INTRODUCTION

The very thought of leading a Bible study need not put the fear of God into anyone. That's the idea behind this book, to take the mystery and fear away from serving as a leader of a small group. Fear not; this book is designed to give you the confidence and skills to be a good leader. If you can read, you can lead.

Using this book, a layperson can teach a Sunday school class with little preparation. It's for anyone who is called on to teach a lesson on short notice. Contained in this book are 52 "stand-alone" lessons appropriate for use in a variety of settings. Each can be used as a one-time lesson for an "in-between week" while waiting to begin a new study or series. Each can also be used by substitute teachers who need a ready-to-use study.

How to Use This Book

Review the titles of the 52 Bible studies listed in the table of contents. They are divided into two groups, 26 by Bible themes and 26 by current issues. Select several that may meet the needs and interest of your small group and choose the one that is most appropriate. This book can also be used for weekly meetings and can provide discussion text and topics for an entire year.

The Purpose of a Bible Study

Much of the confusion and fear of serving as a small-group Bible study leader comes from not understanding what the true purpose of a Bible study is. The purpose of a Bible study is to:

Connect the Bible with daily life
Give participants the opportunity to share their faith
Build rapport with others (group building)
Raise a faith concern that needs to be addressed
Learn more about God by studying God's Word

Dear Lord, They Want ME to Teach the LESSON!

You'll notice that sharing theological expertise is not the purpose of a Bible study. You need not have an advanced degree in theology or be a pastor to lead a discussion group. Your opportunity as a leader is to get participants talking and sharing their faith. Bible study leaders guide their group on its spiritual journey into the Bible. It is your task to get your group started and move them along as best you can. Don't worry about perfection, just focus the group on the Word of God.

Your Homework Before Meeting

Once you have selected a theme or issue from this book, begin your preparation with a brief prayer and meditation about your choice. Ask God to open your eyes and guide you as a leader. Open your Bible and read the text several times. Becoming comfortable with your material is an important first step.

Review your chosen lesson. You'll notice each of the 52 lessons is organized in the following manner:

Bible theme or current issue
Scripture reference
Reflection and summary
Questions for group discussion
Closing prayer

Each Bible study is designed to last from forty-five minutes to an hour. Try to begin and end on time. The authors have used the New International Version (NIV) Bible for scripture quotation. You can use this or other versions of the Bible in your study.

The discussion questions are divided into three sections. They have been designed to encourage participants to talk about their relationships. This is more comfortable than directly asking for their thoughts on the biblical text. You are free to use any or all questions, but try to keep the discussion moving along. Write your own questions about the text if you desire. Close the discussion with the supplied prayer or one of your own.

One Important Note

When class begins, help your participants become familiar with the theme or issue. Give them the opportunity individually

Introduction

to read the scripture text from the Bible. Increase their level of comfort by reading aloud the reflection-summary in this book on your chosen theme or issue. This additional information and background will assist them in answering discussion questions.

CHECKLISTS

Preparation Checklist

__Select one of the 52 Bible studies.
__Pray and meditate.
__Have available a copy of the New International Version (NIV) of the Bible or translation of your choice.
__Review the text summary and discussion questions.
__Bring along nametags (if appropriate).
__Make sure Bibles are available in the classroom.

Bible Study Format Checklist

__Begin on time.
__Introduce yourself.
__Have participants introduce themselves.
__Allow a few minutes for participants to read the scripture for today's lesson from their Bibles.
__Read the text from your Bible aloud to the group.
__Read aloud the summary-reflection as printed in this book.
__Begin with a discussion question. If no one responds, answer the question yourself and then ask participants for their opinions. Remind the group that there are no "wrong" answers.
__Give everyone the opportunity to talk. Some may not want to say anything. Others may want to say everything. Try to find a balance.
__Thank the group for their participation.
__Close in prayer, or ask a volunteer to pray.
__End on time.

26 Thematic Bible Studies

1
A God Who Gets His Hands Dirty
Psalm 23

Psalm 23 is about a God who wants to be part of our lives, no matter how messy or dirty or imperfect our lives are at the moment.

This psalm is attributed to King David. David had no illusions of a distant, sterile God who stayed away from people. One need look no farther than the word "shepherd" (23:1) to find this aspect of God described. Shepherds were filthy dirty. They were survivors in the wilderness. They knew how to live and survive off the land. They could kill bears and lions with little more than their hands or a sling at close range. This God, this shepherd, was one with whom David could relate, for you'll remember that David, too, was a shepherd.

Another thing about shepherds is that shepherds lead others. God leads us in the dark, through the dirt, in the peril of the night, through the darkest valley (v. 4). God gets his hands dirty in the trenches—preparing a banquet for us in the presence of our enemies (v. 5). God gets his feet dirty in the fields, stomping on the grapes to make wine so that our cup overflows (v. 5). God is a God who goes with us where no one else will go. God is a God who fights for us, who fights against enemies no one else can match. God will go wherever we take him, into the abyss, into the darkness of our heart, into the darkest valley of our sin. God is a God who wants to get involved in our lives.

We know from history that God sent his son to get involved for us as well. Jesus died for us, in the sweat and the spit and the blood and the pain and the mess of the cross. He gave his life for us on a garbage dump called Calvary outside Jerusalem. Again, God was getting his hands dirty for us.

We are not the shepherds, the saviors, those who are required to be perfect. That's God's business. God is the shepherd. God is the one who saves, the one who protects, the one who gives life, the one who forgives. We are called only to let God do his job. We are called to let God get his hands dirty in our lives, to let God love us and forgive us so that we might experience the joy of his salvation now, in our lifetime. The Lord is our shepherd, now and forever.

Our Relationship with Family, Friends, and Others

1. Share a time when you have felt alone or afraid.
2. In what ways is God a shepherd to you?

Our Relationship with God

1. In what way or ways can God be part of your life today?
2. In what way has God been part of your life in the past?
3. How is it helpful and hopeful to know that God wants to get involved in your life on a daily basis?

Our Relationship with the Church, Community, and the World

1. In what ways can your church make God's activity known?
2. In what ways do you see God's activity at work, at home, or in the community?

Prayer

Thank you, God, for being involved in our lives daily. Help us to follow your lead and to trust in your salvation. Amen.

2
Finding Room for Jesus
Luke 2:1-20

Even Jesus had trouble finding a place for himself in the world. When Jesus was born, Luke records quite simply that "there was no room for them in the inn" (Luke 2:7). Jesus struggled to find a place for himself growing up. His hometown of Nazareth didn't accept him as a prophet. The religious leaders—his peers in one sense—rallied the crowds to crucify him. Even in death there was no room for him—his body was taken down from the cross and placed in a borrowed cave. It's a puzzling question: Why was there no room for Jesus?

When Jesus was born, his coming did not interrupt schedules. It did not change the lifestyles of the multitudes of people present in nearby Jerusalem. It did not, at least at first, cause a commotion or make people uncomfortable with the way things were going.

It's interesting to note, however, that those who knew about the Messiah in Luke's story all made room for Jesus, and their lives were dramatically changed. To Zechariah and Elizabeth who prayed for a son, God gave them a child named John, John the Baptist (Luke 1:5-23, 57-80). They made room for God to work through their prayers, faith, and blameless living. Mary, the virgin, made room by believing the angel Gabriel, and the Savior began to grow within Mary's womb (Luke 1:26-56). Simeon, the devout man waiting for the consolation of Israel, made room in his heart by believing the Holy Spirit. He went to the temple before he died to see God's Savior (Luke 2:21-35). So too, Anna the prophet, who made room for God through worship, fasting, and prayer, saw God's salvation in the eyes of Jesus (Luke 2:36-38). And then the lowly shepherds, outcast by society, made room by leaving their sheep on the hills of Jerusalem and believing the songs of the angels on high (Luke 2:8-20).

Those who made room, those who were willing to trust God, encountered the miraculous. Those who took time to believe

Dear Lord, They Want ME to Teach the LESSON!

God's word saw the history of the world change in the twinkling of an eye. Those who flashed vacancy signs for the Savior heard the message that the world need not continue as it had been in despair and hopelessness and uncertainty. For God had come to earth to be with God's people. God had come in human flesh to live, and laugh and cry and die, for his brothers and sisters in the world. In the room of these hearts, in the room of those who believed, salvation had come. And so had God.

Our Relationship with Family, Friends, and Others

1. Describe your most memorable Christmas.
2. What do you like most about Christmas in the church?

Our Relationship with God

1. How has the birth of Jesus changed your life?
2. In what ways can you make room for God?
3. Share an idea, practice, or family tradition that makes Christmas more meaningful for you.

Our Relationship with the Church, Community, and the World

1. Debate the following statement in two groups: It's not worthwhile for people to attend church if they come only once a year at Christmas.
2. What special event happens in your community during Christmas?
3. What special gift could you give to your community at Christmas?

Prayer

Dear God, we live in a busy world. Many things clamor for our attention. Help us make room for you in our lives. Amen.

3
One Way
Ephesians 4:1-6

The one way, or most important thing for Paul, is to have a passion for God. It is not a system or a method, but rather an attitude. An attitude where we let God surround us like the bars in a prison and confine us to God's Spirit and salvation and hope and life. This is the one way—through the "one Lord, one faith, one baptism" (v. 5).

"As a prisoner for the Lord" (v. 1), each one of us has been captured by God and given all that is needed in Jesus Christ. The one God who is Lord of all, who works through all, and is in all (vv. 5-6), has given us the one way of salvation. God's one way, God's one desire, is that we become entirely dependent on God for everything.

A loose paraphrase of verses 4-6 could be as follows: "Don't go anywhere else. Go to God. You've got everything you need. Throw yourself completely and unabashedly into the loving arms of God. Abandon yourself to trust in God and let him take care of you. After all, there's only one God, and nothing else comes close. One Lord, one faith, one baptism, one God, who works through all and is in all."

It's perplexing, and yet it's a reality, that even though the one God is in us, we find it difficult to trust God for our needs. Day after day we trust other people with our lives. We trust other drivers in cars. We trust that the airplane we take will get us back safely. We trust people with our investments and our health. We even trust complete strangers. And yet, when it comes right down to it, it's often hard to trust the One who created the universe and spanned the heavens.

This text reminds us of the one God who promises to give us all our needs and who promises never to leave us or forsake us. We don't need less of God, we need more of God. We need so much of God that nothing else will permeate our beings. That is when we'll know the one Way and what it means to have a passion for God, the God who is Lord of all and is in all. Our journey of faith, this one way, begins and ends with God.

Our Relationship with Family, Friends, and Others

1. Share a time when you were utterly absorbed in or committed to something.
2. In what ways do you trust others when going to work, school, or play?
3. Complete the following: "To have a passion for God means..."

Our Relationship with God

1. Would you say you are a "prisoner for the Lord"? Why or why not?
2. Share a time when you trusted God and God responded.
3. When do you find it difficult to trust God?

Our Relationship with the Church, Community, and the World

1. True or false: "God works in my life in more ways than I can imagine." Explain your answer.
2. At what age do you think one stops learning about God and God's blessings? At what age do people start learning about God? Explain your answers.

Prayer

Lord of all, make us prisoners of your love. Surround us with your Spirit and show us the one way, the way of life through you. Amen.

4
Tuning In to God
1 Samuel 3:1-10

The story about God's call to the young boy Samuel reminds us of God's continued effort to reach us and speak to us in a noisy and busy world. God calls each of us, through the Holy Spirit, to tune our lives in to God's strength and power so that we might in turn speak a healing word to others.

Several things stand out about God's call to Samuel. At the end of verse 1 we read, "In those days the word of the LORD was rare; there were not many visions." We get a hint of what this verse means from the wordplay in verse 2. We read that Eli's eyes were so weak that he couldn't see. His vision was poor. Visions were rare (v. 1), but even if they came it was doubtful anyone would see them, especially Eli. We know that Eli did nothing to stop the continued evil of his sons. He didn't carry out God's vision for God's people.

Another thing that stands out about this call is that God's word came to a boy rather than to a high-powered spiritual leader. We think Samuel was about twelve years old when he was in the temple—about the age of a sixth-grader. Samuel later became God's prophet. The key here is not our spiritual training or background, but rather our openness and willingness to trust that God will care for us. Like the boy Samuel, we need to be open and attentive and available to God's word. God is an equal opportunity employer when it comes to giving visions.

It is not always easy to interpret God's calling. Prayer and discernment and help from others are required. The sin that clouds our world and covers God's grander vision of peace reminds us that we do not always listen to God, that we can inflict pain and suffering on others out of selfishness. It is God who gives life its hope and meaning. It is God who shows us the extent of his power and love and healing and forgiveness despite our human actions. Our call is to hear God's word, to let it change us as God wants, and to let it move us out into the world to proclaim God's word of life and salvation.

Dear Lord, They Want ME to Teach the LESSON!

As the boy Samuel experienced, there will be resistance, there will be suffering, there will be human evil, there will be heart-wrenching decisions. But in the end there will also be the peace that God has the final word for life and life everlasting.

Our Relationship with Family, Friends, and Others

1. Do you think God speaks in our world today? Why or why not?
2. Eli helped Samuel discern God's call. How has a friend helped you hear God speaking? How have you helped others hear God's voice?

Our Relationship with God

1. What is your favorite method or place for listening to God?
2. Recall a time when God spoke to you. What was the situation?
3. Tuning in to God requires that we listen. Take a minute of silence now to listen to God. How is God calling you to act?
4. How have your eyes grown dim—how have you taken God's activity in the world for granted?

Our Relationship with the Church, Community, and the World

1. How is your church listening and acting on God's word in the world? (Hint: think of missions, donations, and so on.)
2. Share a time when you risked something (i.e., friendship, your pride, your safety) to share God's word.

Prayer

Ever-present God, open our eyes and our ears so that we might hear your word and respond in faith. Amen.

5
No One Is an Island
Romans 14:7-9

In one of his sermons, John Donne wrote, "No man is an island, entire of itself; every man is a piece of the continent, a part of the main..."

The apostle Paul makes the same claim in his epistle to the Romans, emphasizing the unity we have in Christ. As fellow believers, we do not live alone or believe alone or die alone.

"None of us lives to himself alone" (v. 7). We are a global community. Grain and soybean crops in the United States determine markets around the world. Wars and political maneuvering across the Atlantic Ocean affect the price of oil, and in turn the price we pay for gas in American gas stations. The threat of building nuclear arms across the Pacific in China or North Korea sends warning signals around the world. Actions in our country and actions in other countries have a widespread impact around the globe. Our country is no longer an island, able to act alone. In life, in whatever we do, our lives are strangely knit together.

We are not islands in our individual lives, either. An act of kindness reaches far beyond its initial destination. A caring conversation lasts more than a moment, a kind gesture can last more than a lifetime. We also know that unkind deeds and actions can have lasting effects. What we do as individuals affects our family, our friends, and our community. We do not live for ourselves.

"None of us dies to himself alone" (v. 7). The pain and tragedy of death strike deep and hard precisely because our world will no longer be the same without those who have died. Even after death we are connected somehow. In the Apostle's Creed we declare our belief in the "communion of saints." We do not die for ourselves; our death affects others.

No one is an island to God. The apostle Paul knew Jewish Scripture. He knew that God had not forsaken Abraham, or Moses, or Noah, or Sarah, or Ruth in their time of need. God had not forsaken the Israelites when they persisted in wandering on their own, away from God. Nor did God abandon the apostles, though they fled for their lives and abandoned Jesus at his death. God does not leave us, even in the midst of our sin and deadly ways. The blood of Christ covers us, even as we strive to control our own lives, even as we try to claim independence from God. Even though we want to be islands because of pride and selfishness, God is there in life and in death. For "whether we live or die, we belong to the Lord" (v. 8).

Our Relationship with Family, Friends, and Others

1. "No one is an island." Share something positive or negative someone did that affected your life.
2. Think of someone you know who died. In what way did you feel "connected" to this person?

Our Relationship with God

1. "No one is an island to God." What does this mean to you?
2. In what ways do we keep ourselves separate from God, like islands?
3. Share a time when you felt God's presence.

Our Relationship with the Church, Community, and the World

1. Think of your church and your community. Is your church an island or a part of the community? Explain.
2. What does the phrase "communion of saints" mean to you?
3. Think of three ways you are surrounded by the love of others.

Prayer

Dear Lord, no one is an island to you. Remind us of your lasting, steadfast love that gives us life now and forever. Amen.

6
God Works with Whatever Is Available
1 Kings 17:7-16

The story of Elijah and the widow is set on a stage of desperation. The widow is about to prepare her last meal for herself and her son so that they might die in peace. From literally nothing God provided food for Elijah and the widow's family day after day until the rains came. Their despair was changed to hopefulness. The story of Elijah and the widow reminds us that God works in our lives with whatever we have and whoever we are. God works with whatever is available.

Ahab, the evil king of Israel, had decided earlier to worship the foreign fertility god, Baal, rather than the God of Israel. Elijah confronted Ahab for this blasphemous behavior and said there would be neither dew nor rain in the years to come except by Elijah's word. The word of Elijah held true, and there was no water. Brooks began to dry up. Even the countries surrounding Israel felt the pinch of this imposed drought. It was at this point that Elijah was called to begin his trek to the widow in Zarephath.

Both the country of Zarephath and the widow were strangers to Elijah, yet he trusted God by going on the journey. Elijah interrupted the widow's death processional by asking the widow for her two most precious goods, water and food. The widow, in turn, trusted Elijah, and the food miraculously held out day after day. The prophet and the widow found out that the little they had was plenty. God works with whatever is available.

Though we may not be in the same life or death situation as this widow, there are moments when we, too, feel we are at the end of our rope. We may be alone or feel that there is nothing in the world left for us. We may be lacking the food of love from others. We may feel desperate or ashamed for not having done more with what God has given us. We, too, find ourselves in droughts and famines of our own making.

Dear Lord, They Want ME to Teach the LESSON!

In the midst of a world that refuses to believe in miracles, in a world that says we never have enough, God reminds us that he can work with whatever is available. No matter how desperate the situation, no matter how dry our wells of hope seem to be, no matter how little we seem to have, God continues to work with whatever is available.

Our Relationship with Family, Friends, and Others

1. Share a time when you, like the widow of Zarephath, felt at the end of your rope.
2. Think of a time when you made a huge sacrifice to help someone. What happened?

Our Relationship with God

1. When do you find it most difficult to trust God?
2. When is it easiest for you to trust God?
3. Share a time when God made a difficult situation better for you.

Our Relationship with the Church, Community, and the World

1. Think of a current event in the world that reminds you that God is working despite the odds.
2. Think of a situation in your church or community that seems hopeless. How can God work with what is available for healing or restoration?

Prayer

Faithful God, you can work with whatever is available in our world to give us life and hope. Help us trust in you day after day. Amen.

7
Chaotic Calm
Psalm 46

The refrain near the middle (v. 7) and at the end of this psalm (v. 11) summarizes its theme: "The LORD Almighty is with us; / the God of Jacob is our fortress." God is in control of history, of events, of the universe, and of life itself.

There is no doubt in the mind of the psalmist who is in control. The psalm begins just as it ends with complete trust and faith in God. "God is our refuge and strength, / an ever-present help in trouble" (v. 1). Neither the foaming, chaotic sea—reminiscent of the chaos of Genesis 1—nor the shaking of the earth at its very foundations is a match for the solid, steadfast, ever-present love of God.

The psalmist's faith reminds us of how God has acted throughout history in saving the people of God. In the Exodus from Egypt, God delivered the Israelites from the bonds of slavery. God led them by day in a cloud, and at night by a pillar of fire. Their world, too, was crumbling around them as they fled for their lives from Pharaoh and his mighty army. But they could walk through the middle of the chaotic Red Sea on solid ground because God was there with them, present to help.

God continued his saving work on earth in the person of Jesus Christ. Through Jesus, God continued to be a source of comfort and strength for the sick, the oppressed, and the mournful. The blind were given their sight, the sick were healed, and those who lost loved ones were given the hope of eternal life. But even Jesus was not a guarantee that life would remain peaceful. When Jesus died on the cross his disciples were shocked. Their own lives were threatened, so they hid in fear and confusion. Their world, too, was suddenly chaotic and falling apart. They groped for answers and questioned and doubted what this Messiah, this Savior, was all about.

God is the solid ground on which we can stand in the midst of turmoil. God is our refuge and strength in times of trouble. He comes to us as he did to the disciples in the person of Jesus

Christ. Not to condemn, but to comfort. Oh yes, we will doubt. And yes, we may hurt from the knocks and pains of this world. But in the midst of the world's turmoil is the fortress that refuses to move. "The LORD Almighty is with us; / the God of Jacob is our fortress" (vv. 7, 11).

Our Relationship with Family, Friends, and Others

1. Share a time when your earth seemed to give way. What gave you strength?
2. What is your favorite story in the Bible where God acts to save someone? Why do you like it?

Our Relationship with God

1. What image comes to mind from the words in verse 1: "God is our refuge and strength"?
2. In what ways can God offer stability, or peace, to your life?
3. Verse 10 says, "Be still, and know that I am God." Write down three different ways you can be still, and thus experience God's presence.

Our Relationship with the Church, Community, and the World

1. Do you see the world as a peaceful or a chaotic place? Explain.
2. Circle one of the answers below that best completes this statement, then explain your answer. The church should be . . .
   a. A place to gain protection from the world.
   b. A place to revive us so that we can face the world.
   c. Both a and b.

Prayer

O God, you are our refuge and strength, an ever-present help in trouble. Engulf us with your ever-present love. Amen.

8
What's Love Got to Do with It?
1 Corinthians 13:1-13

God's unselfish, fulfilling love, is the source of all other love. God's love is able to fill us so that we need not fill ourselves with human ambition, empty religion, showy self-sacrifice, or false hopes. God's love is eternal. It is an "always" love that "always protects, always trusts, always hopes, always perseveres" (v. 7).

Although this chapter to the Corinthians is often read at weddings, it was really intended for a much larger audience and a much bigger relationship. Paul was writing to the Corinthian church, a church that was growing. People were excited about God's work and the work of the Spirit. In chapter 12 Paul talks about the different gifts of the Spirit. God has blessed the Corinthian church, as God has blessed all other believers, with various spiritual gifts. Paul mentions some of these gifts as teaching, speaking in tongues, prophecy, and healing.

A problem arose in the Corinthian church, however, because some people claimed that speaking in tongues as a spiritual gift was a sign necessary to prove you were a believer. It was their "acid test," so to speak, to see if others could join their church. If you couldn't speak in tongues, you couldn't join the church.

Paul wrote this 13th chapter to emphasize the true nature of love. It deals with God's love and how that love builds others up. It tells how God's love unifies and brings people together, instead of dividing people into different camps. God's love heals, rather than destroys. God's love accepts, rather than judges. It was a word the Corinthian believers needed to hear as their zeal to promote the gifts of the Spirit divided the church. All people are welcome in God's church.

The apostle Paul's words are a challenge to us all, even though we will never accomplish the kind of perfect love about which Paul wrote. Only God can do that. Only God's perfect love continues to be always patient and kind, unselfish, never rude or boastful, rejoicing in the right, bearing and believing all things, hoping and enduring all things.

God's love is always available as well. God sent his son so that the whole world might be saved. As we open ourselves up to God's perfect love, we in turn can begin to love others. We in turn can begin to see the limitlessness of God's grace. And we in turn can begin to see how the greatest gift of faith, even for God, is this no-strings-attached kind of love.

Our Relationship with Family, Friends, and Others

1. Share a time when you had to do something to join a group.
2. What was expected of you as a child in terms of your faith?
3. When you were a child, was faith something that brought people together, or drove them apart? Explain.

Our Relationship with God

1. Think of three ways in which you have withheld your own love from others in the past week.
2. In what way or ways has God's love brought people together?
3. List three things that remind you of God's continuing love.

Our Relationship with the Church, Community, and the World

1. What are the advantages and disadvantages of having guidelines for people wishing to join groups?
2. What expectations, if any, does your church have for new or existing members?
3. In what ways does the church remind us of God's everlasting, never-ending, unifying love?

Prayer

Loving God, you sent your son to show us the depth of your great love. Fill us with your love and move us to love others. Amen.

9
Rich Toward God
Luke 12:13-21

When we look at the parable of the rich fool, we have no trouble understanding what it means to buy more. Which one of us wouldn't do the same thing if we had a similar bumper crop? Isn't that simply good stewardship?

Jesus' warning in verse 15 ("Watch out! Be on your guard against all kinds of greed; a man's life does not consist in the abundance of his possessions"), as well as the death sentence at the end of the parable, warns us that the bumper crop was not the problem. Notice the self-centered attitude when the farmer talks about his possessions. MY crops, MY barns, MY grain, MY goods. He even consults with himself (v. 19)—rather than God or others—while he makes the final decision. He stores up and prepares everything only for himself.

The ironic thing about the parable is that the farmer has little to do with producing the abundant harvest. Luke writes, "The *ground* of a certain rich man produced a good crop" (v. 16). The farmer may have pulled a few weeds, but overall he was passive in the process. He was given the bumper crop, yet he claimed all the credit.

It's important to note that the parable indicts not those who are rich, but those who place confidence and salvation in the hands of material possessions rather than God. Jesus closes the passage by saying, "This is how it will be with anyone who stores up things for himself but is not rich toward God" (v. 21).

How are we rich toward God? Our richness to God does not lie in taking or in storing up, but in receiving and giving away. Like the farmer, we are passive when it comes to God's generosity to us. We become wealthy by receiving God's harvest of gifts and letting God use our fertile soil of body and soul to bring forth fruit. The challenge is to remember this and to place confidence in God rather than in things.

We have been given much by God. Our task is to utilize these riches as best we can with God's help. It's living each day, mindful and thankful of God's blessings to us, that makes us rich toward God and opens up the storehouse of God's gifts.

Our Relationship with Family, Friends, and Others

1. Think of a person you know who has little material wealth but seems to be happy. What gives that person happiness?
2. Complete the following in groups of three, explaining your responses. "The happiest time in my life was . . ."
3. "You can't buy happiness." In what ways do you agree or disagree with this statement?

Our Relationship with God

1. Write down five blessings God has given you.
2. In what ways can we use our money to help us focus on God?
3. What kind of spiritual investment could you make in order to be rich toward God?

Our Relationship with the Church, Community, and the World

1. In what ways does the world tell us that we are inadequate, or that we need something else to be a more complete individual?
2. What gifts (for example, time, possessions, prayers) can your church give to others in the community or in the world?
3. One way to desire less is to be thankful for what we already have. How does your church give thanks to God?

Prayer

Gracious Lord, help us to be thankful for the gifts and talents you have given us. Assure us of your love and care that we in turn may love and care for others.

10
Wanted: Dead and Alive
Colossians 3:1-4

The apostle Paul doesn't mince words when he talks about life and death. "You died" he says in verse 3, but "have been raised with Christ" (v. 1). The believer is both dead and alive at the same time. We are dead in terms of living only for ourselves. We are dead in terms of what sin has done to us. Yet we are given new life through Jesus Christ. We are given a new mode of operating. Christ does something to us. Something is different about us as the Spirit works in our lives and puts our selfishness to death. Even when our life here on earth is done, death is not the final word. God has given us life and hope in the resurrection.

In many denominations, this passage is a suggested reading for Easter Sunday. The focus is on life. Verse 1 could also read, "*Because* you have been awakened in Christ . . ." Our life is the result of God's work in Christ. Our life does not end in death, but rather begins in death with new life given us by God.

Paul's challenge is to refocus our energy from avoiding death to living life. The challenge is to live as though the resurrection makes a difference. The call is to believe that the death of Jesus still affects us today. The call is to let God worry about our death, rather than fret over it ourselves. The call is to let the resurrection free us so that we can help others discover life rather than avoid death.

Satan wants us to focus on death. That is our sin, a sin as old as Adam and Eve. The sin that believes that we can control the destiny of our very lives, that somehow we have the power to save ourselves from death. The idea that we are trying to deal with death in our own, selfish ways, rather than letting God conquer death for us. Or thinking that God has no part in our lives except when we need God. That is sin. That is admitting that death has the final word.

A more literal translation of verse 3 might read, "For you died, and your life is now hidden in a safe place with Christ in

God." God has a better plan for us than death and sin. God has given us life in the safety and assurance of his son's death and resurrection. The empty tomb reminds us that the message is not to avoid death, but to acknowledge death, realizing LIFE has the final word. "For you died," says Paul, but "have been raised with Christ." We are dead and alive; dead to sin but alive in God.

Our Relationship with Family, Friends, and Others

1. How long do you wish to live? Explain.
2. In what ways has your faith made a difference in the lives of others?

Our Relationship with God

1. Describe a person of faith that is not afraid to die.
2. In what ways have you been awakened, or given new life in Christ? (Hint: think of answers to prayer, faith experiences, and so on.)
3. "For you died, and your life is now hidden in a safe place with Christ in God." Write down what this means for you.

Our Relationship with the Church, Community, and the World

1. Do you think our society spends more time focusing on life or avoiding death? Explain.
2. Think of your worship service. In what ways are you reminded of your new life in God?

Prayer

Living Lord, you have given us life even in the midst of death. Renew us with your life-giving Word and Spirit. Amen.

11
Where's the Other Half?
Genesis 2:4-25

God is in the business of completing relationships. "The account of the heavens and the earth when they were created" (v. 4) begins with nothing on the earth. There were no shrubs, or animals, or human beings. God changes this earthly void by creating the first human being from the dust of the ground (v. 7). God creates a human being in God's image (Gen. 1:27), so that God might love and care for him. From the start, God completes a relationship—part of the divine lies in human flesh. A human being is created in the image of God.

This person, this one who will tend the earth, has been created from the very essence of that which he will work and till. In the Hebrew text, *Adam*—which means "man"—is created from the *adam*ah—"earth." James Limburg, an Old Testament scholar, suggests that "earthling" may be a more fitting name for this close relationship of earth and creature. Again, God completes a relationship. From the earth God creates the earthling.

Before the earthling can speak for himself, God realizes that there is something missing. "It is not good for the man to be alone. I will make a helper suitable for him" (v. 18). God attempts to fill this void of loneliness by creating beasts of the field and birds of the air (v. 19). The earthling now has creatures on the earth and above it, but still "no suitable helper was found" (v. 20). God completes yet another relationship by creating a woman from the man's ribs. Here also the Hebrew is helpful. The woman is literally "built up" from the man's bone. The word "bone" here has a very specific meaning. It signifies that this new person is the very heart of the person from which it came, the same "essence of being." It is bone of bone, flesh of flesh, an equal and perfect counterpart.

God is in the business of completing relationships. Perhaps this is why this biblical text is so popular at weddings. It is equally true for all our relationships, however. God is the one who adds meaning, wholeness, and completeness to our relationships with family, friends, and spouses.

We know from experience that sin alters and separates relationships. Anytime we put ourselves first before God or others, our relationships are less than what they were meant to be.

Sin is not the final answer, however. God is. God is in the business of completing relationships and making us more complete as we let God work in our lives.

Our Relationship with Family, Friends, and Others

1. Would you say that your family is "close"? Explain.
2. True or false: "women and men are equal."
3. Think of a relationship that turned sour. How was sin part of the cause?

Our Relationship with God

1. What do you think it means to be created in the image of God?
2. How has God completed relationships in your own life?
3. Write down a time in the last week when acting selfishly hindered a relationship.

Our Relationship with the Church, Community, and the World

1. In Genesis 2:7, the *earthling* was created from the *earth*. How might this affect the way we treat the earth today?
2. Does faith hinder or help you form relationships with those around you? Explain.

Prayer

Creator God, you formed us from the earth and made us complete. Renew our relationships and fill us with your creative love. Amen.

12
Yo-Yo Christians
1 Kings 19:1-8

The life of faith is one of ups and downs. As we know from experience, the many high points of our faith are accompanied by difficult times. Elijah the prophet discovered the same in his own ministry. He went from a mountaintop high on Mount Carmel to a life-threatening low in a matter of hours. Despite Elijah's inconsistent emotions and feelings, however, God was consistently faithful.

We jump into the story of Elijah with a death threat on his head from Jezebel, the wicked queen. Elijah has just defeated and killed 450 prophets of the foreign god Baal on Mount Carmel (1 Kings 18:16-40). This spiritual victory suddenly turns into a dark valley as Elijah flees for his life (19:3). Even the geography helps tell the story of Elijah's yo-yo emotions. His spiritual high is on Mount Carmel; his spiritual low takes place in the desert below. Elijah goes into the desert, lies beneath a tree, and asks God to take his life (19:4). God does not take Elijah's life, however. God feeds him instead with bread and water, giving him life in the midst of death.

It is clear from the Hebrew text that Elijah is going into the desert to die. He abandons his servant and goes into the wilderness with no thought of returning.

One wonders if this is the same victorious Elijah from Mount Carmel. One wonders if this is the same Elijah who trusted in God to feed him and a widow for three years during the famine, if this is the same Elijah who prayed to God to bring a dead boy back to life, the same Elijah who by faith and obedience was sustained and nourished and protected by the God of Israel.

In many respects, this story of Elijah is not unlike our own. Our ups and downs as Christians confront us daily. Our spiritual highs from a retreat or seminar or Bible study leave us depressed as we return to our work Monday morning. We receive an answer to prayer, but rather than give thanks, we forget about it and turn inward to ourselves and the problems pressing around us. Though empowered by God's grace and promise of life, we fall back to sleep.

The promise of faith, however, is that even though we may be yo-yo Christians with our ups and downs, God is consistently there for us to give us life. Even after we run away from God, God is there to sustain us. Even when we cannot pray, God reveals himself to us. Life comes as we place our faith in God.

Our Relationship with Family, Friends, and Others

1. Share a time when it was difficult to go on.
2. Living out my faith when growing up was: (a) hard; (b) easy. Explain.

Our Relationship with God

1. What's the most exciting faith experience you've had? How long did it last?
2. What helps you get through the "down" times?
3. Write a short prayer thanking God for his continued love, guidance, and salvation.

Our Relationship with the Church, Community, and the World

1. Debate the following statement: "Christians should always be happier than those who do not believe in God."
2. Is it O.K. to be a yo-yo Christian in your church? Explain.

Prayer

Dear God, even though our faith may be inconsistent, your life and salvation are always with us. Lead us with your Spirit to trust in you always. Amen.

13
Everything You Need to Know About Love
1 John 4:7-12

Everything you need to know about love is listed in these few verses from John's Epistle. Love comes from God. God is love. Those who love know God. God first loved us, and not the other way around. Since God so loved us, we should love others.

The Greek root for the word *love* in these verses is *agape*. It is the same word used in 1 Corinthians 13 for love. It is used to emphasize a sacrificial, self-giving love for others.

Note that the focus behind this passage, and really through verse 21, is on whom is being loved. The focus is on the objects of love. For instance, God loves us, where we are the objects of love. In turn, we are to love one another, where those we love are the objects of our love. We need someone or something to fulfill our love.

God also needs someone to fulfill God's love. God needs us to make God's love complete. When we think of the creation story, God created people in God's own image (Gen. 1:27). God needed someone to love. It is true that God had the plants and animals and the heavens and the seas, but God needed human beings for the perfect love God is capable of giving.

We see two things about love in these verses, then. First, that God's love is completed when it is directed to others, when it is directed to you and me. We could call this a vertical love, since it flows down from God. God is the source of love here, loving us freely. God sees beyond our faults and our sinfulness and loves us despite these shortcomings with no strings attached.

Second, we see a horizontal type of love. This is a love that is passed on to those we call on daily, a love that reaches out to neighbor and stranger alike. Strangely enough, however, even this love doesn't begin with us. It begins with God. "Since God so loved us, we also ought to love one another" (4:11). We are like conduits that pass on God's love. As we learn to accept God's love, we in turn can love others. Better yet, as we strive to love those around us, we learn more about God (4:12).

Love comes from God. God is love. Those who love know God. God first loved us, and not the other way around. Since God so loved us, we should love others. That's everything we need to know about love.

Our Relationship with Family, Friends, and Others

1. Who loved you when you were growing up? How did they show their love for you?
2. Can we learn to love, or does love just happen? Explain.
3. True or false: "My God is a loving God." Explain.

Our Relationship with God

1. How can you spend more time with God to learn how to love?
2. In what three ways does God show God's love to you?
3. For you, what is the most exciting thing about God's love?

Our Relationship with the Church, Community, and the World

1. "We need someone or something to fulfill our love." Explain why you agree or disagree with this statement.
2. Write down the name of one person you will love in order to know God better.

Prayer

Loving God, it all begins with your love. Help us become wholly dependent on your love. Amen.

14
Conquerors or Conquistadors?
Romans 8:35-39

The text from Paul's epistle to the Romans is a familiar one. It is often read at funerals because of its strong promise in the midst of adversity. In trouble or hardship or persecution or famine or nakedness or danger or sword, neither life nor death, angels nor demons, present nor future, height nor depth, nor anything else in all creation shall separate us from the love of God. Indeed, it is fitting for such a time as death because it assures us of God's victory for us and our eternal life in God. But it is also a wonderful daily reminder for us that it is God who wins the battles for us. We may want to be the conquistador or victor and try to win our own battles, but it is God who is the conqueror for us.

There is a cartoon of a well-dressed man talking to his pastor. During the conversation the man says, "I want to reach spiritual perfection as soon as possible, then move on to bigger and better things." I believe such a response drives home the question buried in the Romans text. It is one thing to be conquerors in Christ; it is another thing to be self-made conquistadors out to win our own spiritual victories without God's help.

In verse 36, Paul quotes Psalm 44:22. In Paul's time, persecution was a reality. You'll remember that Paul persecuted Christians before his experience on the road to Damascus. In fact, the first Christian martyr, Stephen, was killed at Paul's feet (Acts 7:54–8:1). So when Paul says that they faced death all day long and were considered as sheep to be slaughtered (8:36), it was a statement of reality. People were being killed for their religious convictions. There were definite physical struggles of life and death. But this statement was not Paul's battle cry to raise up a Christian army to defeat an earthly enemy. Rather, it was a reassurance that in all situations God was present. God held the victory for those who believed.

It is often easy to forget God's part in what God wants to claim as a victory, and we instead claim victory for ourselves. We struggle to win the battle alone, to make the conquest a solo rather than a team effort with God. The apostle Paul doesn't applaud such individual effort. He simply says that no matter what happens, we as believers will not be separated from the love of God. We cannot be assured of life, or continued wealth or happiness or safety. But we can be sure that our victory takes place in Christ as we let God work in our lives. We are not conquistadors, but rather conquerors through Jesus Christ (8:37).

Our Relationship with Family, Friends, and Others

1. Should God be involved in your daily decisions? Why or why not?
2. In terms of your own faith walk, were you taught to do things on your own, do them with God, or let God do all the work?

Our Relationship with God

1. Do you think God still has power in the world today? Explain.
2. Share a time you were convinced of God's power.

Our Relationship with the Church, Community, and the World

1. In a war, should we ask God to win the battle for us? Why or why not? What if both sides are Christians?
2. True or false: "People in the community would say that God is working in our church." Explain.

Prayer

Creator and giver of life, we give ourselves into your hands. Help us rely on you and remind us that it is only in you that we receive the victory and crown of life. Amen.

15
Helping Hands
Luke 7:11-17

The story about Jesus raising a widow's son from the dead reminds us of God's healing touch. God cares for us as we live from day to day and hour by hour. "God has come to help his people" (v. 16) and to give life. We, too, are challenged to spread God's message and love with others.

It was common for people in Jesus' time to believe that misfortune or death or illness was God's divine retribution. A parallel story from 1 Kings 17:17-24 shares this perception. A widow in Zarephath whom Elijah the prophet is visiting is sure she has done something wrong and is receiving God's wrath when her only son dies suddenly from an illness. She says to Elijah, "What do you have against me, man of God? Did you come to remind me of my sin and kill my son?" (1 Kings 17:18).

People believed that God punished them for their sins. The raising of the widow's son in Luke's Gospel, however, shows us that the opposite is true. When Jesus saw the grieving mother, "his heart went out to her" (v. 13). Jesus did not come to punish and make life more miserable. He came to save, rather than destroy. He came to heal and mend.

God does not love us for what we do, but for who we are. God loves us because we are God's child, not because we say our prayers or go to church or sing in the choir. The text is silent about the character of the widow, her good works, her spiritual prowess. It says only that her son has died. God loves us because we are part of God's special creation, and we cannot do anything that will keep God from loving us.

People are filled with praise when Jesus raises the widow's son. They shout, "A great prophet has appeared among us!" (v. 16). This response also mirrors that of the story mentioned earlier in 1 Kings 17:17-24. After Elijah brings the widow's son back to life, the woman says, "Now I know that you are a man of God" (1 Kings 17:24). The prophets were God's speakers in the world, and God took an active part in spreading his message through these "mouthpieces."

God still works through individuals today with hands that heal and hands that prod us into service to spread God's message to others. We are to become prophetic. We are challenged to risk ourselves for others. We are called not to give in to death, but to carry out God's word of life.

Our Relationship with Family, Friends, and Others

1. As a child, what was your picture of God? What was God like?
2. Does God punish us for our sins? Why or why not?
3. True or false: "It is easier to believe that Jesus came to save and heal others rather than to heal and save me."

Our Relationship with God

1. Write down three words that best describe God for you. Share these words and their meaning with another person.
2. In what ways has God demonstrated a healing touch in your life?
3. Share a circumstance where you think God prodded you to do something.

Our Relationship with the Church, Community, and the World

1. Are there prophets in our time? Who are they? Explain.
2. Complete the following. "In terms of my faith, the hardest thing for me to live out on a daily basis is . . ."

Prayer

Lord of our lives, heal us with your hands and prod us with your touch so that we can live in service to you. Amen.

16
Living the Question
Matthew 16:13-20

Jesus confronts and challenges us to grow as people of faith with two questions. First, "Who do others say that Jesus is?" And second, "Who do YOU say Jesus is?"

The disciples rattled off the answer to the first question without much thought (16:14). Other people had evidently told them their opinion of Jesus. The second question, however, is much more difficult. You can almost feel the deliberateness of Peter's response. "You are the Christ, the Son of the living God" (16:16). This is no secondhand answer, but rather a confession of faith from the heart. As Jesus indicated, the answer was revealed by God himself (v. 17).

When Peter makes his bold confession of faith that Jesus is the long-awaited Messiah (the Christ), Jesus replies, "And . . . you are Peter, and on this rock I will build my church." For Peter, answering the question meant gaining an identity as a person of faith.

Simon Peter, the fluctuating, impulsive disciple, is given a new identity as the "rock" on which God will build a community of faith. And true to history, Peter becomes one of the leaders of faith in the early church.

Similarly, when we confess God as our God and creator, when we confess the words of our creed, we hear again that we are a child of God, saved and redeemed by the blood of Jesus. God says to us as well, "You are part of the church's foundation built on Christ. You are my chosen, my beloved, sent forth into the world to do my will." Confession of faith gives us identity.

"Living the question" is a phrase Henri Nouwen, the Roman Catholic theologian, used to challenge his students to really take questions of faith seriously. Pursuing questions is a way to grow. "Who do you say God is?" is such a question we need to ask ourselves if we are to discover the riches of God's mercy and power. Is your God big enough to handle all your pain and hurt?

Is your God the God of Scripture who promises to take care of you in all circumstances, in good health or ill, in life and death, in wealth and in poverty, in certainty and doubt?

Asking the question reminds us that our God is a living God, a God who works and exists in history, a God concerned with our existence and future. It reminds us that we have a God who is close at hand, rather than a distant God of the past.

Our Relationship with Family, Friends, and Others

1. Were you encouraged to ask questions of faith growing up? If so, in what ways?
2. Use one sentence to describe who Jesus is to you.
3. If you could ask God one question, what would it be? Why?

Our Relationship with God

1. In what ways is God more than you expected? Less than you expected?
2. Is God able to work in our lives if we have doubt or fears? Explain.
3. List three of the most important things you know about God.

Our Relationship with the Church, Community, and the World

1. In what ways does your church encourage you to ask and explore questions about God?
2. Share a time you learned something important about God. How did it change your outlook on life?

Prayer

Infinite God, help us find out more about you. Draw us close and open up our hearts so that we might live our questions of faith. Amen.

17
Getting Honest with God
Psalm 13

Psalm 13 is about as honest as it gets. The psalmist pours out feelings of loneliness and despair. Underneath the pain, however, is a heartfelt belief that God is there to hear and to respond. The psalmist knows that he can vent feelings of guilt, frustration, anger, and joy to a God who is big enough to handle his pain and loving enough to respond.

The psalmist does not hold back his feelings in this psalm, nor does he waste time doing so. "How long, O LORD?" he begins, "Will you forget me forever? / How long will you hide your face from me? / How long must I wrestle with my thoughts / and every day have sorrow in my heart? / How long will my enemy triumph over me?" (vv. 1-2).

Things are going rough. The psalmist feels abandoned, alone, forgotten. And yet, rather than closing up and keeping quiet, he pours out these thoughts to God. He exposes his secret thoughts, even thoughts that appear to question the very nature of God as he laments, "Will you forget me forever?" (v. 1).

This psalm is known as a lament. It begins with a pouring out of the psalmist's troubles. In the first two verses alone the psalmist cries out to God, "How long?" a total of four times. In verses 3-4 the supplication appears, where the psalmist asks God for help. The psalm ends in verses 5-6 with trust and thanksgiving to God. The psalmist knows that God is trustworthy and will act—he prays to God precisely because he believes God can do something about his situation. So the psalm ends as it begins, focusing on God. The cycle of the lament is complete as it goes from complaining (vv. 1-2) to requesting (vv. 3-4) to trusting and thanking (vv. 5-6).

Though some are hesitant to rail at God, we find out more about God as we do so. We find out that God accepts us for who we are. We find out that God doesn't answer us by saying, "You did WHAT?" We discover that instead of rejection or ridicule there is unconditional acceptance. In the place of anger or fear or guilt we find forgiveness. In the place of thoughts such as "Nobody could ever love me for who I am," we find God telling us that we are of tremendous worth. We are so valuable and so loved that God sacrificed his son for us.

It may not have been easy for the psalmist to share such honest thoughts and feelings with God. It isn't easy for us, either. But as we open our souls, God is waiting to embrace us.

Our Relationship with Family, Friends, and Others

1. "When I feel hurt I . . ."
2. Think of a time you took a risk to share something with someone else. What happened?
3. Discuss the following with another person. "It is O.K. to complain to God."

Our Relationship with God

1. Do you find it easy or difficult to talk to God? Explain.
2. Check all that apply. "Prayer—talking to God—should be . . ."
   ___ focused on the positive.
   ___ focused on God.
   ___ focused on ourselves.
3. What helps you talk to God? What helps you listen to God?

Our Relationship with the Church, Community, and the World

1. Think of your worship service. In what ways do you share your feelings or hurt or pain as a congregation with God?
2. Do you think your church allows people opportunity to share their pain and doubts openly? If so, how?

Prayer

Caring God, thank you for listening to our words of pain and joy. Help us open up to you so that we can discover what a gracious God you really are. Amen.

18
Subversive Joy
Philippians 4:4-7

The apostle Paul's confidence and joy are not based on circumstances, but on God. Even in the midst of trouble Paul can rejoice in God's peace and the Lord's coming.

It might not be surprising to find the apostle Paul writing about joy in everyday circumstances. However, Paul has been arrested for preaching the gospel of Jesus Christ and is spending his time behind bars (Phil. 1:12-14). These words of rejoicing are penned from the depths of a prison cell.

It is not the *what*—things or circumstances—that gives Paul confidence, but the *whom*. Paul places his trust and joy in God. "Rejoice in the Lord always," he writes, "the Lord is near" (vv. 4-5). "Present your requests to God" (v. 6). Paul's focus is on God.

Some people have labeled such joy subversive joy. It is a joy that rests in the claim that the future belongs to God, a God who may come in unsuspected ways and at unsuspected times. It says that God works in surprising ways for us, ways that conquer death and pain and loneliness and isolation. It is a subversive joy because it believes that God is coming again for us, and that even now God is working in our lives to fulfill God's will. We know who is coming and what is going to happen, and because of that we can live with the joy that goes beyond circumstances.

Paul's exhortation to "rejoice in the Lord always" (v. 4) isn't a command, but an invitation. It is an invitation to rest our lives and worries and difficult situations in the care and mercy of God's loving arms. It is an invitation to look beyond our circumstances and to look at the giver of life. It is an invitation to seek the one in whom we can trust our very lives.

Yes, the Lord is near, perhaps nearer than we think, perhaps closer than we know. And he is working in our lives so that we might share not only the hope and joy in our day-to-day circumstances, but the joy of life everlasting. God has come to release us from our prisons. Rejoice, rejoice in the Lord always, in life, in death, in pain, and in health. The Lord is at hand.

Dear Lord, They Want ME to Teach the LESSON!

Our Relationship with Family, Friends, and Others

1. In what ways did you thank God as a child?
2. Should Christians always be happy? Explain.
3. Do you think Jesus' second coming is near? Why or why not?

Our Relationship with God

1. True or false: "God tests us by putting us through trials." Explain.
2. Share a time when you really grew as a Christian. What were the circumstances?
3. Do you focus more on the joy God gives to us in this life, or the future joy promised in eternal life? Explain.

Our Relationship with the Church, Community, and the World

1. What kind of "prisons" at home or work steer our focus away from God?
2. Debate the following in two groups. "The apostle Paul is really saying in these verses, 'Don't worry, be happy!'"

Prayer

Dear God, give us a subversive joy that is focused on you. Thank you for your presence in all our situations. Amen.

19
Big Protection
Psalm 91:1-4

The psalmist offers a picture of a big God who offers us big protection and security. Unlike security made by human hands, however, God's protection does not wear out or deteriorate over time. God's faithfulness lasts not only a lifetime, but into eternal life.

Refuge (vv. 2 and 4), *fortress* (v. 2), *shield* (v. 4), and *rampart* (v. 4) are all used to describe the extent of God's unfailing love. We don't hear the word "rampart" used very much these days. Other translations use the word "bulwark." A rampart is a human-made structure that acts as a protection or defense against attack.

One of the greatest human-made structures used for protection was the Great Wall of China. At nearly 4,000 miles long, it is the longest structure ever built and is one of the only human-made sites visible from space. The walls are 25 feet tall and 25 feet thick at the base. The watchtowers, which are built every 100 or 200 yards, stand 40 feet in height. The top section was wide enough to be used as a road by soldiers and builders. This immense rampart took 2,000 years to build, with work started in 400 B.C. Although it's not being used for more than tourists these days, it stands as a monument of the protection and security it offered centuries ago.

We are more sophisticated these days and don't need a big wall to keep others out. We place our trust in weapons, in diplomatic relations, in science, in medicine, or in knowledge. These have hardly been the final answer, however. Our world is still threatened by the danger of nuclear weapons or the quick escalation of war. Our medical treatments, though more specialized and sophisticated than ever before, cannot cure diseases as common as cancer or AIDS.

Though we continue to build or do things to keep other things or people out of our lives, history teaches us that nothing is indestructible. The Great Wall was crossed by Genghis Khan in the thirteenth century to conquer much of China. Our walls of security will crumble and deteriorate, too, if we place our protection and security in the hands of people. Like the psalmist, we must realize that our ultimate refuge and security rests with God.

God's faithfulness and saving grace surrounds us in life and in death. But unlike the protection developed and built by human hands, God's protection does not crumble or fail. It needs no modification or structural changes as the years go on. There are no cost overruns or budget problems or failure to meet deadlines. God himself has met us and given us the gift of life and life everlasting.

Our Relationship with Family, Friends, and Others

1. Where do you go when you want to feel safe and secure?
2. What is the most secure thing made by human hands?
3. Of what are you most afraid? Why?

Our Relationship with God

1. In what ways did you feel safe with God as a child?
2. Where is a place you feel safe and secure with God? Explain.
3. How have you placed security in things other than God?

Our Relationship with the Church, Community, and the World

1. In what person, place, or thing does the world place its trust or confidence? Why?
2. In what ways has the church helped you discover the security of God's love and faithfulness?

Prayer

God of power, God of might, your faithfulness is our shield and rampart. Help us look to you rather than the fleeting security of our world. Amen.

20
Where Does It Hurt?
Matthew 9:9-13

Like Matthew, the tax collector, God calls each of us, as we are, to be healed and made whole. The requirement is not to be perfect, but to follow.

As a tax collector (v. 9), Matthew was employed by the detested Roman government. Many people who collected these monies or duties abused the position. Such persons were outcast by strict Jews, who would have nothing to do with them. Still, Jesus called Matthew to be his disciple and ate with him and many other "sinners" (v. 10).

The call of Matthew is immediately preceded by the story of the healing of a paralytic (Matt. 9:1-8). Although Jesus heals the man physically at first, he heals him spiritually as well by forgiving his sins. When Jesus dines with Matthew and his fellow tax collectors, there is no physical illness to speak of. Yet, there is need of healing. In fact, Matthew has added a phrase in his telling of the story that doesn't occur in any of the other gospels just to make sure we notice his holistic approach. It's the phrase in verse 13: "I desire mercy, not sacrifice." This phrase from Hosea 6:6 can be translated literally as "I desire faithfulness to God's covenant rather than sacrifice." This was Hosea's reminder to the Israelites that spiritual healing was needed, and not just religious lip service.

The people in Jesus' time needed a similar call. They equated God with fulfilling the law or doing good deeds. In their lives this meant you were saved by what you did, by whom you ate with, and by whom you hung around with. It was a system that boiled down religion into doing things rather than caring about relationships. It was a "religious" but unhealthy faith, one that called for perfection rather than grace.

We can fall into the same trap today if we are not careful. We can mistakingly think that we no longer have need for the healing power of God. Or like the Pharisees in Matthew's Gospel, we can be tempted to judge the spiritual well-being of ourselves and others by outward appearances only (v. 11).

God calls us not to be perfect people, but to be forgiven people. God invites us to be healed, in the midst of our sin, as did Jesus to the tax collectors and sinners of his own time. We are challenged, just as we are, to follow him.

Our Relationship with Family, Friends, and Others

1. In what ways does our culture judge people by outward appearances?
2. How do we judge, or evaluate, other Christians?

Our Relationship with God

1. Do you find it easy or difficult to let God know you need healing? Explain.
2. Complete the following. "I find it hardest to approach God when..."
3. In what ways can you follow God now?

Our Relationship with the Church, Community, and the World

1. Would visitors to your church see an emphasis on God's healing and forgiveness or on God's judgment? Explain.
2. Complete the following. "One place our church needs healing is..."

Prayer

Faithful God, you have called us in our sin. Help us to follow you as you make us whole. Amen.

21
Into the Darkness . . .
Luke 22:39-62

The arrest and betrayal of Jesus is a scene that takes place, and builds, in the darkness of Gethsemane. Jesus leaves his disciples behind to go farther into the darkness to be alone in prayer (vv. 40-41). It is the darkness that lulls the disciples to sleep. It is in the darkness the betrayer finds Jesus and the mob arrests him, rather than during the day (v. 53). It is the darkness that hides the followers of Jesus as they run to save their lives from an angry crowd. It is in the darkness that Peter denies his Lord three times.

But it is also in the darkness that Jesus shines forth as the light of the world. Though others run away from Jesus, he will not run away from them. Though others retreat into the safety of the night, Jesus will continue his walk to the cross. Jesus will not give in to the darkness, for he has come into the world so that evil and darkness will be destroyed forever.

One way to think of the "darkness" is to think of it as our "other side," the side that we do not know or choose not to acknowledge. It is the side where sin and pride and selfishness dwell.

The text uses the darkness, both in the world and in our soul, to illuminate the saving power of God. It reminds us once again that it is God, and only God, who saves. Jesus must be arrested and killed if we are to have life. The darkness is with us, but it will not overshadow the light of the world. Jesus is the light that breaks into the darkness. We are not always able to follow God, but Jesus is. We are not always ready to do God's will, but Jesus is. We are not prepared to die for others, but that is precisely why Jesus came into the world. We are not able to save ourselves—that's God's business. Jesus must be betrayed and crucified—he must go into the darkness—for us, for there is no other way. Our salvation, our life, can only be real if it is entirely in the hands of God.

That is why the darkness is so important. Because it is our own darkness, our sin, that illuminates the power of God.

Like Jesus, we need to be willing to enter into the darkness of the night or the darkness of our souls to meet God. We too, need to let ourselves fall into the saving power of God. For only there will we find life. And only then will we see the light that has overcome the darkness. Jesus' promise is that none of those who follow him will fall away. None of those who trust in his power will be left to die. For the light shines in the darkness, and the darkness has not overcome it.

Our Relationship with Family, Friends, and Others

1. Do you think there is a "dark side" to people? Why or why not?
2. Share with another person the name of a committed Christian you know. Why do you think he or she is committed?
3. True or false: "Most of the people I know believe in God only when it's convenient." Explain your answer.

Our Relationship with God

1. How do you keep your life, or sins, hidden from God?
2. In what ways do you make sacrifices for your faith?
3. Do you think times of testing strengthen your faith? Explain.

Our Relationship with the Church, Community, and the World

1. Share a time when you wanted to stand up for your faith, but didn't.
2. In what ways does your church share God's light in the community or in the world?

Prayer

God of light, shine into the darkness of our world. Illuminate our sins with your grace and mercy. Amen.

22
Risks and Rewards
Matthew 20:17-28

Jesus tells his disciples that the Christian faith involves risks and service. It speaks about giving of ourselves and getting little in return. It speaks about success in terms of what we have given away rather than what we receive.

Jesus begins these verses by laying out the stakes. Just as he did as he began his final trek toward Jerusalem (Matt. 16:21), Jesus plainly tells his disciples what's involved in following him to the cross—death (Matt. 20:19). Again, the disciples fail to hear his message. No sooner has he predicted his death than the mother of the sons of Zebedee comes and asks him if they can be part of the glory in God's kingdom (20:21). It's as though they haven't heard a word! Jesus talks about death and sacrifice and risk. James and John are dreaming about glory and honor and life! They say they are ready to die (20:22), but they are not yet ready to make good their words. For like Peter and the rest of the disciples who vow to die for Jesus, they, too, run away and desert Jesus at the time of his arrest and crucifixion (Matt. 26:55-56). They are not ready for the risks involved.

Why does Jesus call us to a life of sacrifice and uncertainty and risk? Because the risk pulls us away from ourselves. The risk draws us to depend on God. The risk pulls us into the loving hands of Jesus. The risk strips us of what is comfortable and shows us the joy of placing confidence in God. The risk allows us to grow in new and exciting ways.

There are hazards and perils in the Christian faith. We will be asked to take chances, we will find ourselves in uncomfortable situations if we let the Holy Spirit move us into following Jesus. But the rewards are worth it, even if it means killing the sinful self inside us that merely looks after personal interests. Our walk may be a lonely one at times, even as it was for Jesus. For those willing to drink the cup, for those willing to take the risk of letting God give you what is important, for those who

Dear Lord, They Want ME to Teach the LESSON!

will venture into giving their life and desires over to the Holy Spirit, there is life and forgiveness and life everlasting.

Our Relationship with Family, Friends, and Others

1. What sacrifices do you remember making as a child?
2. Complete the following. "Most people follow Jesus because..."
3. Do you think the rewards of being a Christian outnumber the sacrifices? Why or why not?

Our Relationship with God

1. Share a time when you were rewarded for following Jesus.
2. Is it more important to feel comfortable with your faith, or to take risks that may feel uncomfortable? Explain.
3. In what ways can you participate locally or globally to serve God?

Our Relationship with the Church, Community, and the World

1. Should people give as much to the church as they receive? Why or why not?
2. Debate the following statement: Missionaries make more sacrifices to spread the gospel than do other Christians.

Prayer

Dear God, you have called us to a life of service. Kindle and renew our faith in order that we might risk ourselves for you. Amen.

23
New Bones
Ezekiel 37:1-14

Ezekiel's vision in the valley of the dry bones is one of the most colorful and hopeful of his career as God's prophet. A massive pile of dried bones covering a whole valley suddenly comes to life through the breath of God. Lifeless, tired bones take on flesh and blood. They go from death to life, from rotting and wasting away to growing, from separate pieces to groups working together, from silence to rejoicing, from inaction to action. Suddenly despair turns to hope.

Ezekiel writes this chapter during a time of captivity. King Nebuchadnezzar and the Babylonian army have destroyed Jerusalem and have captured the chosen people Israel. While most of the Israelites were kept in the ruins of Jerusalem, the leaders and influential people of Israel were taken away on an 800-mile journey to the plains of Mesopotamia. Ezekiel was one of those uprooted from his homeland and transplanted to this foreign land.

All in all, things are very bleak for the Israelites, and the vision points this out. The graves (v. 12) refer to those exiled, like Ezekiel, who have been trapped in a deathlike situation. They have no family, no possessions, no place to worship, nowhere to be buried in this strange land. The bones represent a state of hopeless death and humiliation. Even the geography is significant, for the people have literally come down from the mountains of Israel—from the peak of happiness—to utter despair in the valleys of Mesopotamia (v. 1).

This vision from the prophet comes as a sign of a future hope and expectation. God promises release from foreign captors, freedom rather than enslavement, a homeland rather than a wasteland, friends rather than enemies, the chance to live rather than the chance to die. Ezekiel's vision tells the people of Israel that they have not been forgotten, and that God himself will make the dry bones a vibrant, living people. "I will put my Spirit in you and you will live" says God. "Then you will know that I the LORD have spoken" (v. 14).

Ezekiel's vision reminds us that when God breathes life into us, the breath of the Spirit pushes us out into the lives of others. We actually gain the power to give life because God is in us. God moves in and through us as God's people by the breath of the Holy Spirit to "pick up the pieces" and put us together again. And not just once, or twice, or three times, but moment by moment. God is continually at work, breathing new life into old, dried out bones.

Our Relationship with Family, Friends, and Others

1. Share a time when you felt uprooted or out of place.
2. When have you felt closest to family or friends?
3. The most important things in life are . . .

Our Relationship with God

1. When do you feel most distant from God's presence?
2. When have you been energized—given new life—in your walk of faith?
3. "I feel closest to God when . . ."

Our Relationship with the Church, Community, and the World

1. What has made the transition to a new home, job, church, school, or community easier for you?
2. In what ways is your church a place of renewal and life? Where are there dry bones?

Prayer

Breathe on me, breath of God. Give flesh to my bones, dear Jesus. Fill me with new life, O Holy Spirit. Amen.

24
Sheep and Goats
Matthew 25:31-46

The story of the sheep and goats is about the nature of God, the one who loves us unconditionally. It is a story about the God who saves us, even in the midst of our sin. And ultimately, it is a story about whom we follow, rather than what we've done.

This parable is not about people who know how good they are. Even the righteous are surprised by the verdict of the king. They too ask God, "Lord, when did we see you hungry and feed you, or thirsty and give you something to drink. . . . When did we see you sick or in prison and go to visit you?" (vv. 37, 39). They have no more knowledge of doing good than the others have of doing evil. You'd think if they spent their life doing nice things they'd at least remember a few of the incidents. But they don't. They are as surprised with the verdict as the goats are. So the parable is not just about people who know how good they are.

This is also not a story that says being good pays off. In other words, we don't earn our salvation by simply doing nice things for others. The apostle Paul writes, "Jews and Gentiles alike are all under sin. As it is written: 'There is no one righteous, not even one; / there is no one who understands, / no one who seeks God. / All have turned away, / they have together become worthless; / there is no one who does good, not even one'" (Rom. 3:9-12). This is not a story about being saved by what we do.

Why are the sheep set on the right of God, the favored side? Why are they saved? The answer lies in whom the sheep follow. The sheep are the ones who follow the shepherd. The goats, on the other hand, do not follow the shepherd. The point of the parable is that salvation comes not from what we do, but whom we follow. Those who are saved are those who are tended by the Shepherd. As Ezckiel writes, "This is what the Sovereign LORD says: I myself will search for my sheep and look after them. As a shepherd looks after his scattered flock when he is with them, so will I look after my sheep. I will rescue them from all the places where they were scattered on a day of clouds and darkness" (Ezek. 34:11-12).

God is the one who provides for our every need. God is the one who seeks the lost and heals the sick. God is even the one who helps us do good. God is the one who helps us feed the hungry and visit the lonely and sick, even without our knowledge of it. Our challenge is to let God be our Shepherd so that on the day of judgment we can hear confidently the words of the Great Shepherd when he says, "Come, you who are blessed by my Father; take your inheritance, the kingdom prepared for you since the creation of the world" (Matt. 25:34).

Our Relationship with Family, Friends, and Others
1. Do you think being good pays off? Why or why not?
2. In our society, who are the sheep? Who are the goats?

Our Relationship with God
1. Think of a time God "found" you. What happened?
2. In what ways do you let God care for you and guide you?
3. What verse or phrase from the Bible has been helpful for you in the past in remembering God's guidance or nurturing? Explain.

Our Relationship with the Church, Community, and the World
1. In what ways can your church provide guidance for the community?
2. How can you get involved with your church to feed the hungry, visit strangers, or give others clothes?

Prayer
Judging God, you have shown us that the way to life is through you. Help us trust our lives to you day after day. Amen.

25
An Uncomfortable Faith
Luke 4:14-28

The message of Jesus, the message of salvation and the kingdom of God, is not a comfortable one. It's not meant to put a permanent smile on our face. It's not meant to fit comfortably into our own belief system. It doesn't promise bliss here on this earth. It doesn't promise to fit into our schedules or make life easier. It does promise, however, to give us eternal life and a God who loves us forever.

Empowered by the Spirit (v. 14), Jesus delivers a simple message in his hometown synagogue of Nazareth (v. 16). He has come to preach the Good News, to heal the sick, to free the oppressed (vv. 18-19).

Jesus centers his message on Isaiah 61:1-2, which he reads from the scroll (vv. 18-19). Here the prophet Isaiah compares the deliverance of Israel from the Babylonians to the Year of Jubilee. For God's people, the Year of Jubilee meant the freeing of slaves, the return of property to the original owner, and the cancellation of all debts (see Leviticus 25). Such would be the freedom and joy to Israel when they could finally return to their homeland as free people. This would be "the year of the Lord's favor" (v. 19).

The people in the synagogue appear to receive Jesus' comments enthusiastically (v. 22). The situation turns sour, however, when Jesus challenges them to actually live out the message. Jesus' cheering section suddenly turns into a lynch mob (vv. 28-30).

The message of the kingdom uproots us. It forces us to ask questions about our own lifestyles. It floods us with issues of priorities and concerns for neighbors. It calls us to preach the Good News to the poor, to free the oppressed, to forget debts, to ask nothing for ourselves but to give away all we have. The message of faith and salvation and forgiveness is anything but comfortable or logical. As Dietrich Bonhoeffer said, "When Christ calls a man, he bids him come and die."

Dear Lord, They Want ME to Teach the LESSON!

Like Jesus, the Spirit is at work within us to empower us to preach the gospel. The Spirit works to squash our earthly and comfortable desires so that God might begin to work as he will, love as he wants, and forgive as he desires. We will still be tempted to get in the way, for the road may seem strange and uncomfortable. Yet it is precisely when things seem uncomfortable that God calls us to follow and trust in him so that he may reset our priorities and give us life.

Our Relationship with Family, Friends, and Others

1. Does being a Christian make life easier or more difficult? Explain.
2. Do you think it's important for people to agree on issues of faith? Why or why not?
3. Do you attend church? Why or why not?

Our Relationship with God

1. Share a time when you did something for your faith that was uncomfortable.
2. In what ways can you put more trust in God?
3. The most important thing to me about my faith is . . .

Our Relationship with the Church, Community, and the World

1. I would rather attend a church that (check one of the following and explain your answer):
   ___ agrees with what I believe.
   ___ challenges my faith.
2. In what ways could your church stretch its faith in terms of its educational program? its community outreach? its global outreach?

Prayer

Dear Lord, give us strength to preach your Word. Empower us through the Spirit to trust in you even when it is uncomfortable. Amen.

26
The Good in Good-bye
John 14:1-12

This text from John's Gospel challenges us to say good-bye to the earthly things we so tightly cling to if we are to greet a new beginning. We must let death work in us so that we might experience life. We must let go of any preconceived notions of how God works if we are to grow in our faith.

The disciples are confused and burdened by Jesus' words that he will be going away to a place where they cannot follow (v. 2). They are saddened by the thought that somehow this special earthly relationship must come to an end. They do not understand the necessity of Jesus leaving them (v. 5) or the necessity of the Resurrection so that they might share in a more meaningful life. In short, they do not see the good in saying good-bye.

There is another opportunity Jesus offers in these verses, and that is to know and discover who God is. "If you really knew me, you would know my Father as well," says Jesus (v. 7). The disciples have already seen God through the person of Jesus. They know that God is one who heals the sick, cares for the oppressed, and loves the unloved. In short, they can begin to describe God by what they know of Jesus. Jesus is God in the flesh, God incarnate.

Saying good-bye is difficult because we lose the security and stability of something familiar in our lives. It's difficult because we are suddenly faced with new situations, with something different. Bidding farewell isn't easy, but it is sometimes necessary. For only after we say good-bye to the things we cling to can we welcome the new possibilities and new beginnings in Christ.

There is "good" in saying "good-bye." For the disciples, it was the discovery of a Lord instead of a teacher. It was finding God instead of an earthly master. It was discovering the gift of eternal life, rather than a fear and panic of death. It was realizing that Jesus had to say good-bye to life, that Jesus had to die and be raised again before he could bring others back to himself. Jesus had to leave his earthly place to prepare a heavenly home for his followers. But it was the good-bye, the death, the separation, that made the other good things possible.

Jesus himself comes to take us with him when we say good-bye to the finite things we now cling to. Jesus himself comes to give us a new place when we say good-bye to those things around us which control us and tie us down. Jesus himself gives us the good in good-bye when he says, "Do not let your hearts be troubled. Trust in God; trust also in me. In my Father's house are many rooms; if it were not so, I would have told you. I am going there to prepare a place for you" (vv. 1-2).

Our Relationship with Family, Friends, and Others

1. Do you like saying good-bye to people, things, or situations? Why or why not?
2. Share a relationship you've been unable to say good-bye to.
3. Think of a situation where saying good-bye opened up new opportunities for you.

Our Relationship with God

1. Saying good-bye means letting God forgive you. What sin, mistake, or situation would you like to say good-bye to?
2. In what area of your life can you place more trust in God?
3. List all the things you know about Jesus. Which of these things describe God? Explain.

Our Relationship with the Church, Community, and the World

1. Why might this text be appropriate for a funeral service?
2. What issues can your church, the community, or the world say good-bye to in order to begin anew?

Prayer

Lord, it is not always easy to say good-bye. Remind us of your continued presence so that we can give our cares and concerns to you. Amen.

26 Bible Studies on Current Issues by Topic

27
Addiction
Learning About Compulsive Behavior

Matthew 6:24

Jesus was talking about choices in this text and what is really most important to us. It is about whom we serve, who is the master of our life. His illustration of the relationship between a slave and a master points out we can't have it both ways. You can serve only one master.

As Christians we have one master, Jesus Christ. He is our chosen master and demands our complete devotion and commitment. We have a responsibility for caring for all he has trusted to us. The earth is our home and we are its caretakers. It is a full-time job. Our time and our possessions belong to God. We are accountable to him. The only problem is that sometimes we forget who God is.

It often begins quite innocently. We get distracted from God's work. That's easy to do in our busy world. With everything that clamors for attention, we begin to lose our focus. Work distracts from church. Alcohol gets used as an escape from an unhappy marriage. People live to eat, to drink, to work, to make money, to serve a civic organization, to enjoy new friends or a hobby. The result is that our priorities change. And life gradually goes out of control.

When an activity or possession becomes a god in our life, when we can't control our actions, we have lost touch with the reason God put us on this earth. When food, gambling, alcohol, or drugs becomes an escape, we need to seek help. We need God's help as well as the help of those people who are trained to change our behavior. Life is tough with all its problems and disappointments. Yet our Master gives us strength to do the work he has set before us. But in order to do that, we need to know what is important, and what is not.

God has given us the world. He gives us our health, our wealth, our time, and our possessions. He has given us loved ones and our friends. They all belong to God, who has entrusted them to our care. It is our choice as to what master we serve.

Our Relationship with Family, Friends, and Others

1. What distracts us from our family and friends?
2. Share a time in your life when you grew distracted or confused about your priorities.
3. How can family distract us from serving God?

Our Relationship with God

1. Why does God want us to have only one master?
2. Name some ways we can be focused on God and doing his work.
3. What are some warning signs that our relationship with God is in danger?

Our Relationship with the Church, Community, and the World

1. Name some addictions or excesses that are common in our world.
2. Why is support an important element of recovery? How can the church provide support?

Prayer

Master, we thank you for all you have given us and done for us. Help us to serve you and remember what is important in our lives and in our relationships. Give us wisdom to know ourselves and learn our limits so that we keep our life in balance with you. Amen.

28
AIDS
Jesus Shows Love to an Outcast

Matthew 8:1-4

The crowds could see him coming and steered clear of him. Some people probably jeered at him and told him to go away. He looked terrible and it made people feel uncomfortable. There was no cure for his disease. People were scared to death of it, and those who had the disease were treated as if they were dead.

The outcast approached Jesus and knelt before him. This was a daring act, because society forbade his contact with others. To touch a person with this disease, or even come too close, would make you unclean. The outcast cried out to Jesus, "Lord, if you are willing, you can make me clean." Jesus responded by saying, "I am willing." Jesus touched him and the man was healed.

Jesus touched him. Those near Jesus must have gone into shock at his gesture. Maybe even the outcast himself was stunned. He hadn't asked to be touched, only to be healed. What Jesus was doing was showing compassion for a man who approached him with faith and in humility. He responded out of a sense of duty and love. Jesus accepted him, not as an outcast, but as a human being. He saw beyond the disease and out of love risked breaking the rules to help.

The disease Jesus cured was leprosy, a terrible illness that isolated and then destroyed. It is a disease that has much in common with AIDS. Victims of AIDS become outcasts, rejected by many at a time when they need love and acceptance. The disease is misunderstood and has many labels and fears attached to it.

We live in a society that is afraid of people who are different from us, who don't look or act as we do. It is a risk to accept, love, and help those whom we don't understand, the outcasts. Jesus took that risk with the leper. He expects us to follow his example.

Dear Lord, They Want ME to Teach the LESSON!

Our Relationship with Family, Friends, and Others

1. Name some ways we can show compassion for people with AIDS.
2. How have you felt the impact of AIDS?
3. Have you talked to anyone about AIDS? What did you learn?

Our Relationship with God

1. How has God provided help for people living with AIDS?
2. How can our faith help in the fight against AIDS?
3. What lessons is God teaching us from the AIDS crisis?

Our Relationship with the Church, Community, and the World

1. How can we promote acceptance of diversity within the church?
2. Is our church a refuge of love and acceptance?
3. What agencies in our community offer AIDS education?

Prayer

Dear God, we thank you for this time together and for this discussion about AIDS. We ask for your healing for those with AIDS and that there will soon be a cure for this disease. Help us to be your hands and your voice in the fight against AIDS. In Jesus' name. Amen.

29
Anger
Consequences and Cures

Matthew 5:21-22

It happened in a suburb of Minneapolis, Minnesota, but it could have happened anywhere. Two cars of teenagers exchange insults at a stop sign. One car arrives at a field and the teens begin a soccer game. An hour later, the second car drives by the field and sprays bullets at the players and spectators. Two innocent bystanders are killed.

Jesus is calling his followers to a higher standard in this text as he warns about the dangers of anger, especially an anger that lingers. It can be deadly. Jesus warns us not to kill others with our thoughts, words, or deeds. Unclean desires can ruin our lives as well as the lives of others.

Our world needs to listen to what Jesus is saying. You only need to read the newspaper or watch a television news broadcast to see the results of lingering anger in our society. Frustrated people take guns to work, to court, and even to public restaurants in an attempt to resolve years of hate and bitterness. Marriages end not only in divorce, but also in murder. It seems that anger is often in control, as well as out of control.

Jesus knew the horrible consequences of unresolved anger, hidden in the heart. His words in Matthew serve as a warning to us today that insults and gossip have no place in the life of a Christian. They are a cancer, which if not cut out, can injure and destroy. Our systems need purging of hidden resentments so that we will not be a slave to anger.

There are cures for anger. Love and forgiveness, which also come from deep in the heart, can transform us and touch others. It isn't always easy. People can be difficult to love. The inconsiderate driver, the annoying neighbor, the gang leader, the egocentric boss, and the thief do have one thing in common, however. Each one is a child of God, just like you.

Our Relationship with Family, Friends, and Others
1. Who or what makes you angry the most?
2. What do you use to control your anger?
3. Can anger ever be healthy?

Our Relationship with God
1. Does anger interfere with our relationship with God?
2. Can we be angry with God? Can God be angry with us?
3. What lesson has God taught you about anger?

Our Relationship with the Church, Community, and the World
1. How does the church help heal the world of anger?
2. Name some issues that cause anger in your community.
3. What should we as Christians be angry about?

Prayer

Dear Lord, we thank you that love is stronger than anger. Please help us rid our hearts and minds of bitterness and hate, which slowly eat away at us. Open our eyes to see others as your children and grant us wisdom to live together as you intended. Amen.

30
Courage
Faith Turned into Action

Matthew 15:21-28

Her neighbors probably thought she was an ordinary woman. In many ways, she was. But when her daughter became seriously ill, this Canaanite woman made a choice. She would do whatever it took to make her daughter well again. And she meant it. Reading between the lines, we might assume that this woman had tried the conventional and even some unconventional cures. Nothing had worked. Then she heard about Jesus and his miracles.

Going to Jesus was not easy for her. She was not Jewish. Women held a low place in society. The disciples didn't want her around. It seems there were more reasons to stay away than to go. Jesus did not encourage her. At first, he didn't even respond to her request. Then Jesus said he was sent only to Israel. She persisted. He compared the situation to giving children's food to dogs. That didn't stop her. Citing her faith, Jesus granted her request and healed her daughter.

It certainly took courage for the Canaanite woman to subject herself to hostility and humiliation. It was her faith in action and her persistence, however, that made her courage pay off. For Christians, this same formula continues to result in miracles in our world today. Faith is taking action. Knowing God is with us gives us courage to do what is right, to do the will of God, and to persist.

It takes courage to live today. The person who gets treatment for drugs or alcohol abuse knows this. So does the victim of an accident. People who take a stand against drugs and crime have courage. To risk confronting someone or just saying "no" isn't easy. Nor is leaving your security behind to try something new. The person in the hospital with cancer or AIDS has courage. It is often easier to die than to struggle to live.

Dear Lord, They Want ME to Teach the LESSON!

When you believe there are no hopeless situations, you have courage. It isn't easy. Courage takes faith, action, and persistence. That's what being a Christian is all about: Knowing God is with us, enabling us to take risks out of love for others.

Our Relationship with Family, Friends, and Others

1. Share a moment of courage from your life.
2. How can love of friends and family give us courage?
3. What situations can cause us to act with courage?

Our Relationship with God

1. Why does God want us to be persistent in our requests to him?
2. How does our faith provide us with courage?
3. Does it take courage to be a Christian?

Our Relationship with the Church, Community, and the World

1. Name some examples of people of courage in our world today.
2. How can the church be more courageous in its mission?

Prayer

Dear God, give us the courage to trust and believe in you. Help us to be bold in our requests to you, knowing that you will respond in love. Amen.

31
Crime
The Good Samaritan

Luke 10:25-37

It was a fairly ordinary robbery, a frequent event on the road between Jerusalem and Jericho. A traveler is attacked by robbers, who take his valuables and leave him in the ditch badly beaten. Later, other travelers, one by one, come to the scene of the crime. The first two, the kind of people who you might expect to render aid, do nothing. The third traveler, a Samaritan, tends to the wounds of the injured man and transports him to a nearby inn for care. The Samaritan tells the innkeeper he will pay the cost of the injured man's care.

The Samaritan was certainly an unlikely hero. Jews regarded Samaritans as an inferior race. The worst insult you could make was to call someone a Samaritan, yet it was a Samaritan whom Jesus used as a model neighbor.

The Samaritan was different from the others. He didn't make any excuses not to help when he saw someone in need. He got personally involved immediately, not waiting for more help to come along. The Samaritan could have told the police about the incident when he got to town; instead he did what he could. That's what God asks of us.

Good Samaritans stop and help those in trouble, regardless of any risk to themselves. If you have ever been a victim, you know how important it is for people to come forward with assistance or as witnesses. And if you have ever come forward to help, you know how much your efforts are appreciated. We need one another more and more as crime continues to increase. People who get involved can be one of the best solutions for a rising crime rate. We can make a difference as one Samaritan did.

God calls us to put our faith into action against what is wrong in our world. He created us with hands to help and hearts to care. That's what being a good Samaritan is all about.

Our Relationship with Family, Friends, and Others

1. How has crime touched your life?
2. Does anyone here know how it feels to be robbed or burglarized? Can you share your feelings with this group?
3. How have you changed your life and activities to avoid being a victim?

Our Relationship with God

1. What are some excuses we may commonly give God for not getting involved?
2. What do we lose when we don't step forward to help?
3. What do we gain when we become a good Samaritan?

Our Relationship with the Church, Community, and the World

1. How can the church join the war on crime?
2. What community organizations are available to help victims?
3. What simple things can be done to make the world a safer place?

Prayer

Dear Lord, we thank you that there are people who do take a stand against crime. Grant us the courage to be bold in helping others who are victims and need our assistance. Open our eyes to see how we can protect ourselves and others as we seek safety in your world. Amen.

32
Decisions
Advice from the Expert

Proverbs 3:5-6

The story is told of a farmer who couldn't keep his hired hand busy. The farmer had him chop wood and thought it would take all day, but the task was done within hours. Later, he had him clean the barn. That didn't take long either. Finally the farmer assigned him to sort potatoes, pulling out the rotten ones. The farmer returned to check on his progress and found the hired hand collapsed in his chair completely exhausted. The farmer asked what had happened and the worker replied, "Making all these decisions has worn me out!"

The process of making decisions can be exhausting. God knows this and offers his help in these verses from the book of Proverbs. It begins with trust, acknowledging that God will lead us toward what is best. We are also advised not to limit our decisions using only our own insights. As humans, we have a limited perception. God sees all and knows all. The second verse encourages us to take action, recognizing God has the answer and will help us. We need to go to God in prayer. It is then God can put us on a path toward what is right.

Just think, we have full and complete access to God's counsel and advice! That's better than all the "experts" in the world. We get the best advice there is and at no cost. We can't go wrong. All we need to do is to come to God in prayer. His advice will come; it may not be right away, but as we pray and meditate something will happen. It may be an idea, or a telephone call. Perhaps circumstances will change. Maybe the last bit of information will fall into place. God works in mysterious ways.

It's also good to remember that we can go to God with any problem. God gives us full access without any limits. His advice is the best on all topics including relationships, child care, workplace issues, auto repair, job hunting, finances, even where to take a vacation. The only limits are the ones that we set, or the ones we create when we do not involve God. That's the problem more often than not. We forget about God and try to go it alone.

God is our partner in life. He is our best friend and advisor, and he knows us better than we know ourselves. Our vision and knowledge are limited. We can't see the future. That's why we need God's guidance to stay on the right path.

Our Relationship with Family, Friends, and Others

1. What is the best advice you ever received from a friend?
2. Name some limitations of asking friends for advice.
3. Recall an important decision you had to make and how you made it.

Our Relationship with God

1. How has God helped you make past decisions?
2. What is the biggest obstacle for you in asking God's help?
3. Recall some advice that you believe came from God.

Our Relationship with the Church, Community, and the World

1. How did you make your decision to attend this church?
2. Why is it important for Christians to be involved in community decisions?
3. What are some poor decisions that have been made by politicians? What influenced their decisions?

Prayer

Jesus, we thank you for being our partner in life and for being available to help us make decisions. Help us to lean on you for answers and advice so that we do what is best. Amen.

33
Diversity
Practicing Acceptance

2 Corinthians 5:16-20

It's been said that if people awakened one morning to find that everyone was of the same skin color, held the same views, and acted identically, new prejudices would be discovered within hours. Over the centuries, we haven't made too much progress toward unconditional acceptance.

In our lesson, Paul is promoting reconciliation. He urges that we regard people no longer from a human point of view, but as Christian brothers and sisters. We are a new creation, not our former selves. Paul writes that we are now ambassadors for Christ. It is a ministry that first begins with being reconciled to God, so we can touch the lives of others.

Paul is giving us a great responsibility. We, as Christians, are to represent Christ to others. Our words and deeds are a reflection, not only on Christ, but on other Christians. And Paul is not saying that we are ambassadors only to people we know or who are just like us; he is throwing the door wide open and including everybody!

The problem is that we do not know everybody; we mostly know people who are just like us, who look like us, and share our same values. These are the people who are comfortable to be around. They accept us and we accept them. It is easier to share the gospel of Christ with these people. They're like us.

Most people don't think they are prejudiced. Maybe some are accepting of everyone. But more often than not, we find reasons to avoid associating with people who make us uncomfortable. Members of street gangs, homosexuals, immigrants who can barely speak English, street people, and the mentally and physically challenged are "different" in appearance and lifestyle. We don't know people who are "different," but what are the chances we ever will?

Dear Lord, They Want ME to Teach the LESSON!

God has created us to be diverse in looks, interests, lifestyles, and beliefs, but we are all God's children. Shouldn't we get to know the rest of our family? Think of some of the little things that can be done to overcome the barriers that separate us. Only then can we become ambassadors of Christ.

Our Relationship with Family, Friends, and Others

1. Tell about a friend who is completely different from you.
2. Recall a time when another person made you feel uncomfortable because of his or her appearance, or lifestyle.
3. How did you first meet some of your friends?

Our Relationship with God

1. How does God encourage us to accept others who are different?
2. How was Jesus a model for accepting diverse people?
3. What do you think God wants us to do to eliminate prejudice?

Our Relationship with the Church, Community, and the World

1. How can more minorities be encouraged to attend this church?
2. Name some issues that cause misunderstandings.
3. How do prejudices get started within a community?

Prayer

Dear God, we thank you for making each one of us unique and special in your sight. Help us to remember that your love is for all people and you accept us just as we are. In Jesus' name. Amen.

34
Ethics
Matters of Trust and Truth

Acts 5:1-11

Arthur Furguson was a successful salesman in the 1920s. He learned at an early age that Americans loved bargains, so he sold pieces of Americana at bargain prices whether he owned them or not. In 1925, Furguson sold a cattle rancher a ninety-nine-year lease on the White House for $100,000. Years later, he sold the Statue of Liberty for $100,000. It also earned him five years in jail.

It pays to be honest when you are selling property. That's what Ananias and Sapphira discovered, a bit too late, in our lesson for today. They were members of the early church, which was rapidly growing and prospering. No one had private ownership of anything. It was all held in common (Acts 4:32). Members would routinely sell property and turn all the proceeds over to the church for distribution to the needy. Ananias and Sapphira didn't do this, however. They kept some of the proceeds. And when questioned about it individually, both lied to Peter. Each immediately dropped dead.

As Peter states, the land belonged to Ananias before he sold it. After he sold it, the money was also his, to do with as he pleased (Acts 5:4). God is Truth and what is untrue makes him angry. In our lesson, Ananias and Sapphira not only lied to Peter, they lied to God. It was a serious matter. They were given no second chances. God judged their hearts and the sentence was death. Their death caused the whole congregation to fear God.

It isn't always easy to tell the truth. We can pay a price for being honest. Fear of rejection or someone's getting angry at us can cause us to be less than truthful in certain situations. The truth can hurt others and us. Whether we exaggerate to impress or lie to make a profit, we lose. We lose in the eyes of God, and we can lose in the eyes of others when our deception is uncovered. On the other side of the coin, a clear conscience accompanies truth along with God's favor. We feel better because we have done what is right.

It comes down to a matter of trust. The question is, How much can you trust anyone who lies or shades the truth? If we cannot expect the truth at all times, what kind of relationship can we have? Our reputation is on the line with God and others through our words and deeds. We know the Truth because God has given us the Truth. It is our choice to proclaim it.

Our Relationship with Family, Friends, and Others

1. What are qualities that inspire your trust in others?
2. Name some jobs where high levels of trust are needed.
3. How can trust be increased among friends or family?

Our Relationship with God

1. Why do we trust God?
2. In what ways do we try to avoid telling God the truth?
3. Why is trust so important in our relationship with God?

Our Relationship with the Church, Community, and the World

1. What happens when there is a lack of trust within a church?
2. Should pastors be held to higher ethical standards than others?
3. What professions are often seen as lacking ethical standards?

Prayer

Dear Lord, you are the Truth and we thank you for showing us how important it is for us to be truthful in our dealings with you and all others. Grant us courage always to have high ethical standards, even when it is not easy. And help us remember that there is always forgiveness available when we fall short of the truth. In Jesus' name. Amen.

35
Focus
Looking to God

Matthew 7:13-14

A few years ago, several carpenters were shingling the roof of a farmhouse. In the midst of their work one of the crew noticed that the three-year-old son of the farmer was climbing one of the ladders to the roof. The crew became alarmed. They knew if the boy looked down he might fall two stories to the ground. A carpenter reacted to the situation by calmly and cheerfully encouraging the boy to look up and see what they were doing as he continued to climb. The boy never looked down. He was grabbed and carried to safety when he reached the roof.

It isn't a roof, but rather a narrow gate that Jesus is talking about in our lesson for today. He exhorts us to focus on entering by the narrow gate. Jesus says that many people take the easy route in life. It's a gate that leads to destruction. He encourages us to take the tougher, more difficult way because it leads to life.

Life is tough, yet Jesus isn't trying to make it tougher. What concerns him is the choices we make and our focus in life. Each day we make hundreds of choices, all of which determine our path. Our work, household chores and home, family, friends, and church all vie for our time. How do we maintain a Christian focus?

Like the boy on the ladder, perhaps we need to keep looking up in order to make it safely to our destination. We need to focus on Jesus. The way to Jesus is the narrow gate, perhaps doing what others are not willing to do. That might mean getting up early to read the Bible and meditate before work. The narrow gate might lead us to a nursing home or hospital when we would rather be outdoors golfing. To focus is to stay in touch with God and go where he leads us.

There will always be distractions along with tough choices, but Christ has promised he will be with us on our journey. He'll help us focus on the narrow gate.

Our Relationship with Family, Friends, and Others

1. Name a friend or family member who helps you focus on what is important. If you can, give an example of how this person helps.
2. Name activities that distract us from relationships.
3. Name a time in your life when you lacked focus.

Our Relationship with God

1. How does God help us learn to focus?
2. What are some "wide roads" people take in life?
3. What signals does God give us when we are on the wrong road?

Our Relationship with the Church, Community, and the World

1. What are some symptoms of a church losing its focus?
2. What is often the focus of the news media in reporting community events? Why?
3. What happens when the world is unable to focus on an issue?

Prayer

Jesus, we focus on you because you have redeemed us and given us a new life in you. You are our help and our salvation. Guide us through the narrow gate and encourage us in love for one another. In your name. Amen.

36
Friendship
Loyalty: Ruth and Naomi

Ruth 1:10-18

Clearly, Ruth did not want to leave her mother-in-law, Naomi, after the death of their husbands. Naomi, an Israelite, and Ruth, a Moabite, were living in the land of Moab at the time. Famine had devastated the area. Naomi decided to return to Bethlehem because she had heard the Lord was blessing the land with good crops. Her Moabite daughters-in-law started to return with her, but Naomi persuaded Orpah to go back to her mother's house. Her other daughter-in-law, Ruth, insisted on remaining with Naomi.

Ruth's loyalty to Naomi was shown in the choice she made. It would certainly have been easier to stay with her own people than to move to a foreign land. Women had no status then. The prospects for two older women making such a journey were risky. And there were no promises life would be better in this new land. The only promise was that they would be together.

Life has a way of testing our loyalty to those important to us. We struggle with our emotions when distance threatens to separate us from someone we have grown to love. Loyalty causes us to want to hang on, like Ruth and Naomi. We don't want our level of comfort to change. Best friends don't come along every day, so we want to keep things as they are.

It's been said that a friendship is a gift from God. Friendships are not planned. They arrive out of the blue, evolving over a period of time, sometimes born of common interests, sometimes not. Our friends help us face life's challenges and brighten our days. Like Ruth and Naomi, there is a loyalty that is born from time spent together.

Perhaps God wants us to remember that loyalty has no boundaries. Whether friends are present with us or not, loyalty does keep us together. Life's many demands today may make holding a friendship together tougher than it was in the days of Ruth and Naomi, but the need for friends remains unchanged. God cares about people through people. That's what friends are for.

Our Relationship with Family, Friends, and Others

1. What feelings occur when loyalty is tested in friendship?
2. Why is it so difficult to say good-bye to a friend?
3. What are some qualities of a healthy friendship?

Our Relationship with God

1. What does it mean for you to have Jesus as a friend?
2. Name other pairs of friends that are mentioned in the Bible.
3. What part does God play in friendships?

Our Relationship with the Church, Community, and the World

1. Can Christians and non-Christians be friends? Explain.
2. How does involvement at church encourage friendship?
3. Name some keys to making new friends.

Prayer

Jesus, we thank you for our friendship with you and for the friends you have given us. Help us to treasure our friends, to learn how to make new ones, and to give of ourselves to others. Open our eyes so we can see those who need a friend that we may share your love. In Jesus' name. Amen.

37
Healing
In the Hands of God

Matthew 8:14-15

A few days before he died, John Adams was visited by Daniel Webster. Webster relates that during their conversation a friend stopped by and asked Adams how he was. Adams replied, "I inhabit a weak, frail, decayed tenement; battered by the winds and broken in upon by storms, and from all I can learn, the landlord does not intend to repair."

It is troubling to be sick. A person does not know how long the illness will last, or if good health will return. Sickness also puts us out of commission. It sidelines us from life. We are relegated to bed to pass the time, take medicine, and wait for the illness to pass.

Such was the situation for Peter's mother-in-law. Our text tells us she was sick with a fever in her cottage when Jesus arrived. In those days a fever was serious; many times it was fatal. Jesus took the woman's hand and the fever left her. She then got up and served her guests.

She wasn't the first person Jesus had healed that day. Verses preceding tell us about a leper and the servant of a centurion. Unlike these others, however, this healing was not public. It was done in the privacy of a cottage for a woman who evidently didn't even request healing. It was a display of the kindness of Jesus, ending the suffering of a woman. There was no talk about faith, just compassion and healing.

The mother-in-law's response was gratitude, demonstrated through service. Her health made it possible to meet Jesus' needs and those of other guests. She was healed and was now eager to get on with life.

Stories of illness do not always end so happily. When we are sick we are in the hands of God. He heals for his purposes and in response to prayers. God heals through doctors, but sometimes they are at a loss to help. When people are sick, we can pray for their health and support them, thus helping to reassure them they are loved by many and by a God who cares.

Our Relationship with Family, Friends, and Others

1. Tell about a time when you were ill and a friend helped cheer you.
2. How has prayer supported you during an illness?
3. How do people sometimes change once they recover from a serious illness or brush with death?

Our Relationship with God

1. What lessons can God teach us while we are ill?
2. How can we be more accepting of God's will when sick?
3. How can visiting the hospitalized be good for both the visitor and the person being visited?

Our Relationship with the Church, Community, and the World

1. What are some ministries where the church is engaged in healing or helping the sick?
2. What activities and people are needed to heal communities?
3. How can Christians help heal people in distant nations?

Prayer

Dear heavenly Father, you are the Great Physician. We thank you for the healing you bring to this world and that you care for both body and spirit. We pray for those who are ill that they may be restored to health. In Jesus' name. Amen.

38
Persistence
Requests to a Father

Luke 18:1-8

It was a Saturday morning, and Andrew, age three, wanted to help his father prepare breakfast. His father was going to make omelets and was a bit wary of having Andrew near eggs. But Andrew persisted and his father said he could help, as long as he was careful. Things were going well until an egg accidentally crashed to the floor. Andrew fled the kitchen in tears at the moment of impact. His father asked him to come back and help, and they both cleaned up the mess together. The father was impressed with the maturity and sincerity of Andrew's apology. And Andrew still wanted to help, again to the point of persistence. The father gave in and soon they were back at work. A few minutes later, the fall of a second egg marked the end of a helping hand in the kitchen.

It's difficult to turn down the request of someone you love. That's one of the lessons of the parable Jesus told about the hardhearted judge and the poor widow. It was the persistence of the widow that finally got the judge to grant her plea, not out of love, but because she was a nuisance. The point Jesus was making was that if someone who doesn't even care about a person will grant a request, just think about how a loving Father will listen to the requests of his children.

This parable is about prayer, and it also tells us much about the merits of persistence. It's because God knows what is best for us that he grants what we need, not necessarily what we want. We may want a brand new car, when in reality we only need dependable transportation. God knows the difference when we don't. That is where the elements of patience, determination, and persistence come into play. It's a way of getting us to really think about what we want and why we want it.

God is not a magical genie who automatically grants our wishes. He reminds us of his power and who is in charge as we wait for answers to prayer. For God to give us all we ask would be like a father granting a child's every request. We often forget that "wait" and "no" are sometimes the best answers to prayer requests.

We are loved by our heavenly Father, who answers the prayers of his children. It is our persistence in honest prayer that gets results. And don't worry about being too persistent. Have you ever heard someone regret praying too much?

Our Relationship with Family, Friends, and Others

1. Tell about someone you know who is a persistent person.
2. Tell about a time you were persistent in going after something and your results.
3. What makes it difficult at times to be persistent?

Our Relationship with God

1. Why did God give us the ability to be persistent?
2. Name a time when God was persistent with you.
3. Why is it wise to ask God to guide our persistence?

Our Relationship with the Church, Community, and the World

1. Where does the church need to be more persistent?
2. What is the result when churches are persistent in prayer?
3. In what area could this community be more persistent?

Prayer

Dear Lord, thank you for giving us the ability to stick with and pursue our desires. Help us not to give up, but to seek your will so we go after what is best for us. Allow us to be persistent in service to others so that we further your kingdom. In your name. Amen.

39
Possessions
Living in the Land of Plenty

Luke 12:13-21

The man in this parable may not be much different from any of us. He worked hard, had a comfortable home, enough food to eat, and had a pretty good life. He was called rich, perhaps just as all Americans would be called rich by someone living in Africa. The point is that things were going so well the rich man decided he was going to retire and live off his possessions. It wasn't a wise decision.

That night, the man died. He turned out to be a rich fool because all his possessions were now of no use to him. The man had been rich in property, but poor in his relationship with God. He mistakenly thought the surplus was his. There was no thought of God or sharing his wealth with the less fortunate. His possessions owned him, which was his downfall.

This parable is much like the story of the poor man in a small town who lied to his brother in another state about how wealthy he was. His letters said he was doing great and owned many stores where he lived. Panic set in when his brother decided to visit. The people of the small town decided to make the poor man appear as rich as he had said he was. Storefront signs were changed, and when the brother arrived, the town's people played along with the charade. The plan went well until robbers kidnapped the poor man and held him for ransom. His appearance of wealth almost caused him to lose his life. You don't have to be rich to get into trouble.

There is a fine line between who we are as Christians and what we own. Whether we are rich or poor, possessions can ruin us if we do not have a rich attitude toward God. For rich and poor alike, it is a matter of knowing what is important, and what is not. Jesus warns us in his parable to be careful of wealth. He doesn't condemn wealth, but he reminds us it can get us off track, so that we forget why God put us on earth, to be a servant to others.

A person's life is more than possessions. Treasures accumulated on earth will remain here long after we are gone. They will go to others and eventually decay. It is when we are rich toward God that we are truly wealthy.

Our Relationship with Family, Friends, and Others

1. Tell about a gift that became a prized possession to you.
2. Recall a time that a possession was the subject of an argument.
3. Name a possession of yours that is admired by friends or the possession of a friend that you admire.

Our Relationship with God

1. Would you like God to make you very wealthy? Why?
2. What qualities does a person need to handle wealth wisely?
3. Why is it hard to remember all we have belongs to God?

Our Relationship with the Church, Community, and the World

1. Does wealth help make a church more effective in ministry?
2. What insights about wealth can be found in this lesson that can be applied to communities?
3. When does great wealth begin to be destructive to a person?

Prayer

Jesus, we give you thanks for all you have given us, remembering it all belongs to you and is only ours for a short time. Grant us wisdom so that we keep a proper perspective concerning our possessions. Help us to share what we have with others. Amen.

40
Power
The Calming of the Storm

Matthew 8:23-27

"What kind of man is this? Even the winds and the waves obey him!" This was certainly an appropriate question after what had just happened. Jesus and his disciples were in a boat on the Sea of Galilee. According to another narrative of the same incident in Mark 4:35-41, Jesus had been preaching from the boat to large crowds on shore. It had made him tired, and he had fallen asleep. A violent and sudden storm arose. Jesus kept on sleeping. The high waves threatened to swamp the boat. In terror, his disciples woke Jesus. He calmed the sea and winds to the disciples' awe.

The storms of life can still strike us without warning today. Whether we are driving our car on the freeway, are at work in our office, or are relaxing in the shelter and comfort of our home, life can be turned upside down in an instant. A loved one becomes hurt. We are fired from our job. We lose our health suddenly. Fire, crime, or an accident changes our world in minutes. It is in these times we seek shelter in Jesus. We seek his power.

There are many types of power in our society—political power, the power of the press, judicial power, the power of wealth, just to name a few. Power is what people strive toward. To have power is to be in control. And yet there are so many things in this world that we are powerless to control. It is in these times we seek Jesus.

Jesus has power over disease, doubt, despair, and disaster; over all the storms that threaten us. We know instinctively to go to God in times of trouble. Like the disciples, we have only to ask. Some action on our part is required. We pray for relief. And Jesus brings calm. He calms our hearts, our fears, our minds. The peace of the Lord can get us through any situation. It leaves us in awe.

Dear Lord, They Want ME to Teach the LESSON!

George McDonald has observed, "How often we look upon God as our last and feeblest resource! We go to him because we have nowhere else to go. And then we learn that the storms of life have driven us, not upon the rocks, but into the desired haven."

Our Relationships with Family, Friends, and Others

1. Share a time when you felt powerless.
2. What people are sources of power in your life?
3. Name a lesson you learned about power while growing up.

Our Relationship with God

1. Name a time you felt the power of God.
2. As a Christian, what kind of power does God provide to you?
3. Name some hymns or liturgies that use the word "power."

Our Relationship with the Church, Community, and the World

1. In what ways do you see God's power in your church and community?
2. What are symbols of power for the world?
3. Name some powerful people in your community. How did they get to be powerful?

Prayer

Dear Lord, thank you for being a source of power and strength for us. As you give us power, grant us the wisdom to use it wisely. Remind us that your power brings peace and calm to our lives. In Jesus' name. Amen.

41
Prayer
God Listens to Us

Matthew 7:7-11

With the troubles of the world on her mind, a young girl was saying her prayers at bedtime. After praying for friends, family, and many of the nation's ills, she turned her thoughts to God. "And please, God, take care of Yourself. If anything happened to You, we'd all be sunk."

God enjoys hearing from us and listens to our needs. That's one of the points Jesus was making in our lesson for today. Jesus encourages us to have an active prayer life; to ask, to seek, and to knock. Our requests are heard by a loving Father who wants to give his children good gifts. All we have to do is ask.

It's important to keep asking and not get discouraged, because God answers our prayers in the way that is best for us. We have a Father whose timing is perfect and who knows the right time to respond to our requests. Waiting for an answer can also be beneficial. It tests our desire and can clarify our thoughts. Some of our prayers may require cleansing as they evolve over time. The more we pray, the more clear our prayers can become.

Jesus tells us also that God's answers are based in love. He responds in our best interests, although as children we may not like the answer. Being turned down or told to wait can be difficult. It's not done out of a lack of love. Our prayer requests can be denied for the best of reasons. It might be what we ask could harm us, or something better will come along. The passage of time is often helpful in evaluating former prayer requests. Many a Christian has been thankful what was prayed for never came to pass.

Prayer continues to be the most powerful form of communication in our world today. It changes lives. It brings us closer to God and feeds our soul, allowing a Father's love to penetrate our lives. We ask, we seek, we knock; and God opens the door to his kingdom.

Our Relationship with Family, Friends, and Others

1. How can prayer enhance our relationships with others?
2. Recall a time you were prayed for by others or you joined with others to pray for someone.
3. What person has influenced your prayer life the most?

Our Relationship with God

1. How does prayer bring us closer to God?
2. How does God help us to pray?
3. Recall how you felt when God answered one of your prayers.

Our Relationship with the Church, Community, and the World

1. Name some current world events that deserve our prayers.
2. How does prayer unite Christians around the world?
3. Brainstorm some ideas of who can be our prayer partners.

Prayer

Dear Lord, we thank you for the gift of prayer. Help us remember it is always available to give us direct access to you. Thank you for answering our prayers in our own best interests. We ask you to remember those whom we name in our hearts before you now. Amen.

42
Pride
The First Shall Be Last

Luke 14:7-11

Have you ever noticed how quickly the best places to sit are taken? People attending a movie, sports event, or concert vie for seats with the best view. The most comfortable chairs are the ones occupied first at a party. Children fight for the best seat in the family car. Adults often reserve a window seat on a plane. And special pews are often reserved at churches for weddings and baptisms.

It's nothing new. Jesus noticed this trait in people almost two thousand years ago. He addressed it by telling a parable about sitting at the foot of the table so that the host may ask you to move to a place with more honor, not less. He warned that those who exalt themselves will be humbled, but those who humble themselves will be exalted.

It's a matter of pride, one of the seven deadly sins. It is pride that destroys friendships, causes marriages to crumble, sparks gang violence, kills Christian faith, and makes people think they can get along without God. Being proud isolates us. It causes us to believe we deserve more and better. The focus is on ourselves, and slowly we forget about everyone else, even God.

Jesus calls us to replace pride with humility. That begins with a realistic view of ourselves as sinners, no better than anyone else and deeply in debt to God. As we make ourselves less important, we become more important to God and others. Humility frees us to focus on friends, family, and strangers, as God intended. Humble people realize their own limitations and how much they don't know.

Henry David Thoreau said that humility, like darkness, reveals heavenly lights. Such was the observation of Theodore Roosevelt after viewing the heavens before retiring one night. He gazed at the stars and then told his soldiers, "I guess we are now small enough to go to bed."

Dear Lord, They Want ME to Teach the LESSON!

Our Relationship with Family, Friends, and Others

1. Recall an experience when you were humbled.
2. How can friends and family help keep us humble?
3. Tell about someone who you believe exhibits Christian humility.

Our Relationship with God

1. Name some lessons God has taught you about pride.
2. Name some examples of pride exhibited appropriately.
3. Who are the victims of people with too much pride?

Our Relationship with the Church, Community, and the World

1. What are warning signs of too much pride within a church?
2. How can community pride get out of hand?
3. Give some examples of how pride has caused wars in the past.

Prayer

Dear Lord, you served as an example of humility for all of us. Help us to follow your example and eliminate the sin of pride in our lives. Give us pleasure in giving credit to others. Help us to be realistic about ourselves so that we please you and are better able to help those around us. Amen.

43
Priorities
Eliminating Distractions

Philippians 3:12-16

The great philosopher Henry Thoreau had a problem. He wanted to write a book, but the many details of life kept getting in the way. He kept getting distracted from his goal. Thoreau finally arrived at a solution. It was to move to a cabin deep in the woods. Two years later, he emerged from seclusion with his completed book. He found it pays to keep your eyes on the prize.

Paul, in his letter to the Philippians, advocates a similar strategy in furthering the kingdom of God. In verse 14 Paul writes, "I press on toward the goal to win the prize for which God has called me heavenward in Christ Jesus." Paul had one objective, proclaiming the Good News of Jesus Christ. It was his passion, his single focus in life. And he didn't let anything get in the way.

It was Christ Jesus who motivated Paul. He wrote the Philippians that he kept pressing on toward his goal because Christ had made him his own. Paul knew he was not alone. He walked with Christ each day of his life. Prayer helped him communicate with God and focus on the work to be done. Paul was cheered on by other believers in the faith and encouraged by God's love. It helped him win the prize.

There are few priorities in life, but many distractions. It is difficult to focus on what is important and let go of the rest. That's why we need God's help and the support of other Christians to stay on target. The Lord has given each of us a purpose in life, which needs to be our priority. Like Paul, we need to forget what lies behind and look ahead.

Living a life that is pleasing to God and following his will is our priority as Christians. We can't do it alone. We need to be powered from above. It is the love of God in Christ Jesus that not only breathes life into our lives, but helps us reach our destination.

Our Relationship with Family, Friends, and Others

1. What are some of your family priorities?
2. What are some tests of what are priorities and what are not?
3. How can friends help us set priorities?

Our Relationship with God

1. How can we make prayer and Bible study more of a priority?
2. How does God teach us about priorities?
3. How do our priorities change when we become a Christian?

Our Relationship with the Church, Community, and the World

1. Why is church attendance a priority for a Christian?
2. What are some current community priorities?
3. What world issues are priorities for Christians?

Prayer

Dear Lord, we thank you for this time together to discuss our priorities as Christians. Grant us wisdom to know your will and use our time wisely. Show us how we can be more effective Christians and increase our love for one another. In Jesus' name. Amen.

44
Safety
Peter's Angel

Acts 12:6-11

Is anybody safe nowadays? Whether you live in a small town or large city, fear is on the increase. Drive-by shootings, murders, rapes, burglaries, and bombings are making Americans take cover for their lives. To protect themselves, they are buying more alarms and handguns. Trust is decreasing. As Christians, we look to God for answers.

The situation was just as bleak for Peter. He had been jailed by Herod as a popularity ploy. Now a company of sixteen soldiers were guarding him in a maximum security prison. Peter was chained to two of his guards, hand-to-hand. Outside the prison, Peter was being prayed for by the church. They were looking to God for answers.

God responded with an angel. Peter didn't believe it at first and thought it was a vision or dream. His chains fell from his hands and the angel walked with him past the guards and to freedom. Once he was free, Peter knew it was for real. He praised God for the miracle that had taken place, for a safety that no one could take away.

Two thousand years later, God is still protecting his own. Bullets miss intended victims. People near death recover from their wounds under the skilled care of doctors. Cars that seem destined to collide miss each other at a busy intersection. Witnesses step forward to identify and testify against criminals. And people still escape from deadly situations against all odds. It's not just in the movies. It's real and it comes from God.

Safety will always be an issue. We still must look to God for our help and salvation. As Christians we can always remember:

The light of God surrounds me;
The love of God enfolds me;
The power of God protects me;

Dear Lord, They Want ME to Teach the LESSON!

The presence of God watches over me.
Wherever I am, God is.
That's safety.

Our Relationship with Family, Friends, and Others

1. Name some people in your life who make you feel safe.
2. How do you feel when you do not know if someone is safe?
3. How do we try to protect the ones we love?

Our Relationship with God

1. Name a time when you felt God's protection.
2. Why is God always safe to talk to?
3. What have you learned from God about safety?

Our Relationship with the Church, Community, and the World

1. How can we as Christians make our community safer?
2. What makes a church safe as a sanctuary from the world?
3. What makes our community a safe place to live?

Prayer

Dear Lord, we thank you for protecting us and those we love against all harm and danger. We pray for the safety of those in danger at this moment. May they feel your presence. Help us to rid our nation of crime and violence so that our streets and homes can be safe again. In Jesus' name. Amen.

45
Simplicity
Less Is Often More

Matthew 6:19-21

Buddy, a four-month-old puppy, was alone in the kitchen one morning while his owner slept. The peace and quiet of the house was suddenly interrupted when Buddy began barking loudly and furiously. His owner rushed into the kitchen to find Buddy in the midst of a terrible confrontation. He was barking at his bone.

Buddy lives a simple life. He owns a bone and wears a collar. His food dish and water dish are kept filled and he receives love and attention. That's all he needs. You have to admire that.

In our lesson, Jesus says we don't need many earthly treasures. They usually end up merely causing us problems. Our treasures break, rust, lose their value, gather dust, and cost us money to insure. Thieves can steal them, or our treasures can steal our time from us so that we forget about what really matters.

Jesus has a better idea. He encourages us to store up treasures in heaven where they will be safe. The real treasures in life can include charitable giving, time spent reading the Bible, visiting a friend in the hospital, smiling at someone, paying a stranger a compliment, or taking some kids to the zoo. Acts of kindness have an eternal value. We'll remember and enjoy them forever.

Our closets full of clothes, two cars in the garage, collection of antiques, powerful computer system, home and yard are going to be ours for only a short span of time. In the long run, they really don't matter. It's the simple things, even trying to live with less, that give us more and enrich our lives.

The choice is ours. We can name our own treasures and keep our lives simple. How much do we really need? The less we have, the more time we'll have for what's important. As Jesus says, "For where your treasure is, there your heart will be also."

Our Relationship with Family, Friends, and Others

1. Name some simple pleasures you enjoy with family and friends.
2. Share some activities and belongings that sometimes take away from time with friends.
3. Recall an act of kindness another person did for you. How do you feel about it today?

Our Relationship with God

1. What treasures has God given us to share with others?
2. Discuss the simple life that Jesus led and his lack of possessions.
3. What things does God provide to sustain life?

Our Relationship with the Church, Community, and the World

1. What is the view of the world concerning the needs of life?
2. Compare the benefits of being active in large and in small churches.
3. What can individuals give to a community besides money?

Prayer

Dear Lord, we thank you for the simple things in life, the things that are free to us and those things we can give freely to others. Help us to want less and give more. Teach us to use what we possess to further your kingdom. In Jesus' name. Amen.

46
Talent
Blessed to Be a Blessing

1 Corinthians 12:4-11

It didn't look like much. The owner had cast it away because he thought it had no value. It was an ugly slab of rock, spoiling in a quarry until an artist came along. Using his creative imagination, he saw what the piece of marble could become. He put his talent to work and with patience spent many days chipping away at the stone. The artist was Michelangelo and his creation was his famous statue of David.

Life is a matter of using your talent and imagination. In our lesson, Paul talks about our gifts, given to us by the Spirit. Gifts of faith, of healing, of prophecy, of miracles, and so many others come to Christians for use in the work of the church. Paul tells us that each gift is for the common good and is activated by the Spirit. He speaks of varieties of services and varieties of gifts, all given by the same God.

To other people, we may not look like much. Our flaws are evident. But God doesn't see us as others do. His imagination sees our potential, our talents, what we can become. Like a great artist, God molds us and shapes us into works of art. It isn't done overnight, but over a lifetime. God makes our talent come alive for use in his kingdom.

The talent God has provided comes with obligations. Paul encourages us to use our gifts to help others. Spiritual gifts are made for giving, just like Christmas presents. Whether we teach, heal, write, sell, manage, or repair, our talent is meant to be a ministry to others. It's part of God's plan. As Christians, all our talents fit together. Like musicians in an orchestra, we make beautiful music when we are in harmony with God, with others, and using our talents to their utmost.

Dear Lord, They Want ME to Teach the LESSON!

Thank God for your talents. Praise him for what he has given you. Nurture your gifts so they glorify God. Ask to have your imagination unlocked so that you can see the potential you and others have been given. Together, we have been blessed by the Spirit to be a blessing to others.

Our Relationship with Family, Friends, and Others

1. Name a talent you have that gives you pleasure.
2. Name a gift or talent you discovered in yourself as a child.
3. What gifts do family or friends have that you admire?

Our Relationship with God

1. How do we use our talents to serve God?
2. How does God encourage us to develop our gifts and talents?
3. What does God do when we do not use our talents?

Our Relationship with the Church, Community, and the World

1. What gifts or talents is this church most in need of now?
2. What gifts can the church give to the community and world?
3. What gifts are necessary for leadership in the church?

Prayer

Dear heavenly Father, we thank you for the many talented people who touch our lives. You have blessed us with many gifts. Help us to use them wisely and for furthering your kingdom. Grant us eyes to see the gifts of others and to offer encouragement for their use. Amen.

47
Temptation
Matters of Choice

James 1:12-16

To be human is to be tempted. We are tempted to eat too much, to stay out too late, to stay in bed in the morning, to lie, to call in "sick" for work, and the list goes on and on. What are we to do? In the words of Mark Twain, there is a solution. He says, "There are several good protections against temptations, but the surest is cowardice."

Luckily for Christians, there are other ways to deal with the issue of temptation. James provides some wonderful insights. He says that those who endure temptation are blessed by God and will be rewarded with a crown of life. God gives us this incentive to resist temptation. James points out that it is not God who tempts us, but rather our own desires. The problem is within us.

James tells us temptation is a result of our own sinful nature. It begins with our desires that lead us away from God. We start to focus on ourselves and our wants. Before we know it, sin has entered the picture. It all may be so innocent at first, perhaps merely the stray thought, "Wouldn't it be nice if . . . ?" Our thoughts and desires eventually lead to our actions. That is how sin sneaks up on us.

Temptation is too much and too powerful for us to handle alone. We need the help of Jesus Christ. It is through prayer that we can get the strength to do what we know is right. Knowledge of the Bible, being able to recite verses, is also a power source.

With God we are safe from temptation. That doesn't mean we won't be tempted. Even Jesus was tempted. God does give us strength to resist, but it is our choice. With God's help we can learn to surrender to him instead of temptation.

Our Relationship with Family, Friends, and Others

1. Recall a struggle you had with temptation.
2. Why is it that we are all vulnerable to different temptations? Or are we?
3. Share some of your strategies for fighting temptation.

Our Relationship with God

1. What has God taught you about temptation?
2. What should we do when we lose a battle to temptation?
3. Can temptation ever result in good?

Our Relationship with the Church, Community, and the World

1. What are some strong temptations for churches today?
2. How do the ways of the world tempt us?
3. What community organizations exist that help people fight temptations in the form of addictions?

Prayer

Dear heavenly Father, we thank you for this discussion of temptation, for the sharing of ideas and experiences. Help us to enlist you in our struggle to do what is right. Grant us courage when it is easier to be a coward. Help us remember that your love and support is always with us. In Jesus' name. Amen.

48
Time
Christian Time Management

Romans 13:11-14

A man was telling a group of friends about his concern over his ex-wife's becoming "overly religious." To illustrate her behavior, the man cited the message on her telephone answering machine at home. Her message to callers was, "Today could be your last day on earth. You could die tomorrow. Have you accepted Jesus Christ as your personal savior? Please leave your message after the beep."

Although such a message may go a bit too far, the apostle Paul in our text also expresses his concern over the shortage of time. He wasn't worried about how soon he might die. Paul was anticipating the Second Coming of Christ and wanted the church to be ready. Like Paul, the church was expecting Christ to return at any moment. They believed there was not much time left to proclaim the gospel. Church members were encouraged to have all their personal and business affairs in order because a new beginning was near.

Christians today are still anticipating the return of Christ, but perhaps with less urgency. The end of the world may not seem as imminent. The work of the church continues. The gospel is proclaimed. But it is still only a matter of time until all this comes to an end. As humans, we know our days are numbered and each one brings us closer to death, the grave, and eventually the resurrection. That's why time is so precious. We don't know how much remains.

Paul encourages us to use our remaining time wisely. He calls us to refrain from worldly temptations and lists several sins to avoid. As Christians, Paul wants us to be different from others, serving as an example of what it means to have a relationship with Christ. For us today, Christian time management can include regular study of the Bible, enjoying our family and friends, exercising to maintain good health, serving as a volunteer to help the less fortunate, and making God the center of our lives.

You don't need a message on your answering machine reminding callers they might die tomorrow. Many valuable days and years may be ahead for most of us. What's important is to share God's love in the time that remains.

Our Relationship with Family, Friends, and Others

1. Name a family member you would like to spend more time with.
2. What are some ways you spend time with friends?
3. If you could spend less time at any activity, which one would it be?

Our Relationship with God

1. How does God help remind us that time is precious?
2. How much time does it take to build a good relationship with God?
3. How was the ministry of Jesus an example of good time management?

Our Relationship with the Church, Community, and the World

1. What benefits are there in giving of our time to the church?
2. If you could go to any place in the world and offer your help, where would you go?
3. What prevents people from getting more involved in community affairs?

Prayer

Dear God, you have given us the precious gift of time, and we thank you for the years you have given us. Help us to treasure our time, use it wisely, and give of it freely to people who need us. May we grow closer to you as time goes by. In Jesus' name. Amen.

49
Tomorrow

Looking Toward the Future

Romans 8:38-39

Two caterpillars were crawling across the grass when a beautiful butterfly flew over. One nudged the other and said, "You couldn't get me up in one of those things for a million dollars!"

At the time, the caterpillar didn't realize that it was its destiny to be a butterfly and travel by air. It had a bright future. As Christians, we also have a wonderful future waiting for us. We are children of our heavenly Father, destined for eternal life as sons and daughters of God. In our text for today, Paul saw that it was inevitable we are going to be with God. It is because nothing can separate us from his love.

We need to remember our destiny. At times we are like the caterpillar, crawling in the dirt and weeds of life. We are troubled with illness, bills to pay, relationships, our work, and the necessities of life. All of that is going to come to an end. Our future is with God, who loves us more than we can imagine.

Nothing can separate us from God's love. Death can't touch us, nor can the troubles of this life. God is with us for all our tomorrows. He knows our needs. He knows our names, for they are written in his Book of Life. Our past, our present, and our future belong to God. In his love, Jesus has been with us all along and continues to walk beside us. And he'll be there when we cross over into eternity.

As Christians we can live each day with the certainty that we will live forever. That puts a whole new meaning on life. It allows us to take risks for others as we do the work of our Father. It helps us remember that problems and sadness are temporary. There will always be a tomorrow, because we are children of God.

Our Relationship with Family, Friends, and Others

1. How does knowing our destiny affect our relationships?
2. Name a family member or friend who has influenced your life.
3. In what ways can we control our future?

Our Relationship with God

1. Name ways in which God helps us along in life.
2. How has God shown you his love this past week?
3. How can we prepare now for our future with God?

Our Relationship with the Church, Community, and the World

1. What changes would you like to see in the church in the future?
2. How can the church assist our changing community?
3. How does the world affect the future of the church?

Prayer

Dear Lord, we thank you for all our yesterdays, todays, and tomorrows. You have blessed us with your love and we thank you for leading us forward toward the day we will be with you. Grant us wisdom to use wisely the time you have given us. In Jesus' name. Amen.

50
Trouble
Moving Our Mountains

Mark 11:22-24

There once was a man who had to cross a big hill each day on his way to town. Each time he reached the top of the hill, he would pick up a rock and carry it with him to the bottom. When he was asked why he did this, the man replied he was moving the hill so that one day it would be gone.

This man believed he was moving a hill. Jesus says we can move mountains if we have faith in God. That's quite a statement about the power that a Christian has through prayer. Jesus says it is a matter of faith. If we believe what we say will come to pass, it will happen. Jesus tells us not to doubt in our heart, but have faith. He is saying Christians have the ability to do anything.

It's been said that one way to stay happy is to enjoy trouble. There is plenty of it around. Troubles are like mountains that block our path on the road of life. We come to a mountain of trouble and need to make a decision what to do about it. It may be a troubled relationship, a problem at work, or maybe an illness. Whatever it is, it stops us in our tracks.

Jesus tells us to pray when we are faced with a mountain. The trouble we are facing can be moved out of the way through faith. Our Lord says to believe without a doubt. He doesn't put any limits on our requests, but only asks for faith. He promises to show us a way around our mountain or to move it entirely. The message is that trouble is no obstacle if we only believe.

Faith does move mountains. Christians continue to prove it. We have the power to meet any challenge in life because God has told us how to do it. Pray. Believe. Do not doubt. That's all it takes to conquer our troubles.

Our Relationship with Family, Friends, and Others

1. How has God helped your family face a difficult problem?
2. How can we help others who are in trouble?
3. What happens to relationships when there is trouble, such as an illness?

Our Relationship with God

1. How does God use trouble in our lives to strengthen us?
2. Recall how God helped you escape from trouble.
3. What troubles do we fear the most? Why?

Our Relationship with the Church, Community, and the World

1. Why is there so much trouble in the world?
2. Name some severe community troubles that currently exist.
3. What church resources are available to those in trouble?

Prayer

Dear Lord, we thank you for our troubles because they challenge us to lean on you for help. Thank you for this discussion and for bringing us closer together through sharing our ideas and experiences. We ask your help for those who are troubled, that they may find answers through you. Amen.

51
Unemployment
Advice for Survival

Luke 16:1-9

The story is told of a sixty-four-year-old man who became unemployed during the Great Depression. Unable to find work, he took a tent and a few hundred dollars and moved to the mountains. He built a cabin there and put his imagination to work, finding thirty-six ways to earn a living. His income sources included selling vegetables from his garden, acting as a guide for tourists and hunters, building rustic furniture, serving as a newspaper columnist, and producing medicines from mountain herbs. Six years later, he left his mountain with thousands of dollars and rich memories.

It is this kind of imagination and instinct for survival that Jesus was commending in his parable about a dishonest accountant. The man's employer fired him, but on his last day on the job the accountant took time to make some friends who could help him in the future by reducing their accounts owed.

Jesus wasn't praising the man's ethics. Instead, Jesus was making a point about being practical and resourceful. The accountant knew how to get ahead in the world, or at least stay afloat. Jesus was saying he wants his followers to have this zeal in furthering his kingdom on earth. Christians need to be sharp and on their toes in order to move ahead.

Christians, whether employed or unemployed, can take some lessons from the accountant. He was realistic. The man knew digging and begging were out of the question, so he faced his situation in a practical manner. It was an all-out effort. He used his time wisely and made a plan based on facts. The accountant used his ingenuity for survival.

God wants us to approach life in the same manner as we search for a job, feed the hungry, raise funds for the church, proclaim the Good News, and do the work the Lord has set before us. Being shrewd and passionate are good qualities for a Christian in any situation.

Our Relationship with Family, Friends, and Others

1. If you have ever been unemployed, recall some of the feelings of being in that situation.
2. How can a friend offer support to an unemployed friend?
3. Once you are unemployed, what are some of the obstacles to re-entering the job market?

Our Relationship with God

1. In what ways can unemployment be a blessing from God?
2. Do Christians have any advantages in looking for work?
3. How can God help you find another job?

Our Relationship with the Church, Community, and the World

1. How can church members help those who are unemployed?
2. What community agencies offer help to the jobless?
3. How can we as Christians help unemployed people in other states?

Prayer

Dear Lord, we thank you for giving us work to do for you and others. Help us to remain useful and give us confidence as we face an uncertain job market. Grant us patience when we need work and help us to give support to those who have yet to find employment. In Jesus' name. Amen.

52
Worry
Consider the Lilies

Luke 12:22-31

Jesus gives his disciples some practical advice about life in this passage from Luke. He tells them of a Father who knows all their needs and provides what is needed to sustain life. There is no need to worry about anything. God has it all under control. Jesus is encouraging them to open their eyes to see a creation that receives loving care from its Creator. Instead of worrying, Jesus wants them to focus on the work at hand and let God deliver the necessities of life.

What Jesus is saying is that their view of life is too small. They need to see the "big picture" and learn that life is more than food and clothes. Jesus wants them to see life as something different from a race for the most and the best. Don't imitate the world. Rely on God instead, replacing worry with trust. Jesus tells them there is nothing to be gained from worry. The bottom line is that they matter to God and he will take care of them.

Do not worry. The words of Jesus come to us today in a world that still hasn't received the message. We fret about our computers, cellular phones, automobiles, not to mention the basics of food, health, shelter, and employment. Most people worry about not having enough money, regardless of the size of their bank account. It seems that life has become more complicated, so there is more to worry about. Maybe that is true, but still most of our worries never come to pass. Perhaps the real problem is that we often forget what really matters and what does not.

Deadlines, appointments, and projects are important, but too often it seems they have too high a priority. We worry about them at the expense of our real valuables. It is easy to get too caught up in the world and get in so much of a rush that we forget about God. We worry instead of pray, thinking about ourselves instead of others.

Dear Lord, They Want ME to Teach the LESSON!

God has answers for all our confusion. He tells us that we matter to him and all our needs will be met. His plan is perfect and as we follow Jesus we can become the "worry-free Christians" God wants us to be.

Our Relationship with Family, Friends, and Others

1. Whom do you worry about the most?
2. How can worry affect your relationship with others?
3. What is more productive than worrying about your health?

Our Relationship with God

1. What can we learn from Jesus in this text?
2. What have you worried about that never came to pass?
3. What needs has God met for you today?

Our Relationship with the Church, Community, and the World

1. What issues does your church worry about?
2. How can Christians demonstrate their faith to others?
3. What world issues should the church be concerned about?

Prayer

Jesus, we thank you for showing us what is important and what is not. Grant us strength so that we may replace our worries with faith in you. Open our eyes so that each day we may see your gifts and remember your care for us. Amen.